Cutting Costs
Creatively
A Self-Guided Program for
Continuous Improvement Work Teams

by

Louis E. Tagliaferri

Talico Developmental Systems L.C.
4304 Blue Heron Dr.
Ponte Vedra Beach, FL 32082
904-285-7757
www.talico.com

"Always assume that people are vitally interested in the quality improvement process. They will act to fulfill your conviction."

Philip B. Crosby

Table of Contents

PREFACE

Cutting Costs Creatively is a detailed blueprint for a team effort on the part of the management and employees of an organization to achieve continuous improvement in costs, quality and productivity in all aspects of the business or operation. The program involves a process of analysis, planning, training and problem solving that will help improve overall organizational effectiveness and increase the respect that the organization's products or services command within its industry. At the same time, the program will tap the full creative and innovative potential of all employees as it builds and strengthens teamwork and collaboration within the organization.

The program has four major objectives:

- To develop a consciousness among all employees which makes active, continuous improvement a regular part of planned management and work activities at all levels of the organization;

- To achieve increased organizational effectiveness and profitability by establishing a work climate that is characterized by continuous improvement, full attainment of customer expectations, teamwork, problem solving, and measurement and analysis of work processes;

- To involve all employees in the creative and innovative processes that best facilitates cost, quality and productivity improvement;

- To facilitate the process by which management and non-management employees work collaboratively toward the attainment of a common goal, ensuring the continued strength and vitality of the organization.

The initial focus of the book is the skills and techniques that are the essential tools for a Continuous Improvement Team (CIT) program. However, the book also presents a detailed outline of a CIT program that can easily be adapted to the needs of most organizations together with a Model CIT Master Plan that has the following principal components:

Assessment

A preliminary analysis is conducted within the organization to collect data about the various human, technical and administrative systems that can impact on a CIT program. The total organizational climate is evaluated, prospective CIT targets are identified and the leadership and team skills necessary to successfully implement a CIT program are assessed.

iii

Planning

A CIT Policy Team is appointed to establish program objectives, determine the structure and scope of the program, assign responsibilities and monitor results. This team also develops a master plan to ensure the continuous success of the program.

Team Development

The CIT Policy team selects priority quality improvement targets and appoints problem solving teams consisting of employees from various organization levels and functions to deal with these issues.

Training

CIT team leaders and team members are thoroughly trained in CIT methods and techniques. Emphasis is placed on team building, communication improvement and in the development of creative problem solving skills. The training program is highly participative and focuses on learning through practical application.

Problem Solving

After the completion of training the CITs begin working on quality problems within their assigned target areas. They identify specific opportunities for quality improvement, set realistic, measurable improvement goals and proceed to tackle priority issues using their newly developed problem solving skills.

Support Systems

The CIT program also involves a system of improved organization communication and a system of shared recognition for accomplishments. In addition, the program ensures that the required technical support and interdepartmental cooperation are available in order to effect CIT quality improvements that are approved by management.

This book can be used as a stand-alone self-instruction guide (self-tests will be found at the end of most units of the book) or as a training manual for a facilitated continuous improvement skill development program. We hope that all readers benefit from the information presented in this book and we wish CIT members and leaders and other members of the organization and its management every success in their efforts to continuously improve organizational costs, quality and productivity.

Unit 1   **TOTAL QUALITY AWARENESS**

This unit has two learning objectives:

1. To introduce you to the concepts of total quality awareness.

2. To make you aware of the importance the process of total quality improvement has to you and your organization.

THE CONCEPT

Prior to World War II, and for several years thereafter, The United States enjoyed preeminence as the leading industrial power in the world. During this period the quality of American-made products was matched only by the pride and craftsmanship of American workers and the pride that was taken in the "Made in America" label. Those who were born before 1960 remember with pride the top quality products that were produced in this country including solidly engineered automobiles that were the best in the world, household products like appliances that seemed to last forever, reasonably priced, quality-built housing, highly crafted furniture made by skilled American garment workers, and more. They also remember when foreign-made products like Japanese radios, cigarette lighters, toys and even automobiles were considered to be cheap, inferior products. But then things began to change.

During the cultural revolution of the 1960s and 1970s America lost considerable ground in both the productivity of its workers and in the quality of its products and services. In 1970, for example, the United States had the lowest productivity growth rate among the top 21 industrialized nations of the world. By the mid-1970's it was clear that the quality of goods and services produced in America was headed in the same direction. In more recent years the American economy has reeled under a relentless attack by foreign competition, most notably from China. This has been an attack that has resulted in the loss of hundreds of thousands of jobs, high unemployment, a steady reduction in the quality of life for millions of people, and the purchase of American landmarks by foreign interests.

Serious competition from foreign business organizations can be traced back several decades to Japanese business executives who were willing to listen to the message of an American quality expert, Dr. W. Edwards Deming. In the late 1950's Deming traveled to Japan, as the guest of the Japanese Union of Scientists and Engineers (JUSE), to help rebuild Japan's devastated war economy. He did this by giving quality improvement lectures to executives, engineers and managers. Deming focused his message on statistical quality control and his now famous 14 Points for total quality improvement:

1

1. Create constancy of purpose for improvement of product and service.

2. Adopt this philosophy and aim to take on leadership change.

3. Do not depend 100% on inspection to improve quality levels.

4. Stop awarding business for price only.

5. Improve the system of production and service.

6. Institute training.

7. Adopt and institute leadership.

8. Drive out fear.

9. Break down and eliminate barriers.

10. Eliminate slogans and exhortations.

11. Eliminate numerical quotas for the work force.

12. Get rid of barriers that rob people of pride in what they do.

13. Encourage education and self-improvement for all.

14. Take action.

Regretfully, although Deming's ideas were widely and enthusiastically embraced in Japan, they fell on deaf ears in the United States.

However, since that time a collective concern for quality has arisen throughout America. Faced with damaging foreign competition and a battered economy, leaders in business, industry and government finally began to listen to Dr. Deming and to other prestigious quality authorities like Joseph M. Juran and Philip B. Crosby. Then, in 1982 Congress passed legislation for the formation of a national conference to address the issue of declining productivity and quality. From this was born the Malcolm Baldrige National Quality Improvement Act (1987) and the subsequent establishment of the Malcolm Baldrige National Quality Award (named after the late U.S. Secretary of Commerce).

The Malcolm Baldrige National Quality Award is now presented each year to organizations that meet demanding performance criteria in seven focal areas: leadership, information and analysis, strategic quality planning, human resource utilization, quality assurance, quality assurance results, and customer satisfaction.

Most, but not all, of these criteria are shared by the Deming philosophy. What is shared in common are these essential concepts:

- Total quality means fully meeting customers (internal and external) needs and expectations.

- Total quality is the key to superior organization performance.

- Superior organization performance is essential to organizational profitability and survivability.

- Total quality can only be achieved through a collaborative process of commitment, teamwork, and problem solving guided by the proactive leadership of top management.

- Total quality is a continuous process that is dependent upon effective human resource utilization including work force education, training, skill development and the sharing of appropriate rewards for the achievement of success.

- Each member of the organization, at whatever level, is personally responsible for achieving total quality with respect to the product or service he or she produces.

These criteria are now widely accepted as the definition of total quality improvement, or, as it is also called, total quality management. They have been further refined and embodied in the various quality criteria established by the International Organization for Standardization in its worldwide accepted quality standards such as ISO 9000, ISO 14000 and ISO 27000. Together, these standards for quality, cost containment, productivity and continuous improvement also serve as the foundation for the Continuous Improvement Team program presented in this workbook.

The CIT program combines the most important resources of any organization, the dedicated, responsible men and women who make up the organization, people resources, with the technical and creative problem solving processes that can achieve continuous improvement. It focuses on commitment to quality improvement, teamwork, customer satisfaction, personal responsibility, education, training, skill development and problem solving -- all the ingredients necessary for an organization to improve product and service quality on a continuous basis. The program benefits organizations by resulting in better quality, lower costs, increased productivity and greater profitability. And, it benefits employees by offering them an opportunity to develop new skills, become involved in job-related issues that affect them and by creating a more interesting, challenging job environment.

In operation the CIT program involves setting up teams of employees within an organization to solve quality-related problems. The teams consist of employees from whatever levels or functions of the organization that will enable the best combination of skills to be brought to bear on the assigned cost, quality and productivity-related problem. Both team members and team leaders are trained in effective team problem solving methods and techniques.

The relationship of the CIT program to the concept of total quality is clear. It is designed to create an ongoing awareness of the need for continuous organization-wide efforts to reduce costs and improve quality and productivity. The team process together with its collaborative problem solving effort is at the very foundation of the total quality concept. CITs concentrate their efforts on removing barriers that inhibit an organization from fully meeting customer expectations. And the ongoing nature of the program is fully consistent with the principle of constancy that is the landmark of continuous improvement of product and service quality.

As a result of the renewed commitment of American businesses to continuous improvement in costs, quality and productivity there has been a sharp increase in the quality of American-made products such as automobiles and in labor productivity during the period 2000 to 2010. Today several models of American-made cars are among the best in rated quality. The productivity of the American worker now ranks among the highest among the top 16 industrialized countries in the world and America is regaining some of its lost industrial competitive advantage.

Still, many challenges to the future growth of American business and industrial organizations continue to exist. Increased government regulation, higher taxes and increased global competition require that in order to remain competitive in the world markets American business organizations must launch innovative and creative initiatives to further enhance business profitability and survivability. Today many of organizations recognize the contribution that CIT programs can make to this effort.

TEST & DISCUSSION QUESTIONS

1. In terms of productivity growth, America has continuously been the leading industrial nation in the world since the end of World War II.

    ☐ a. True

    ☐ b. False

2. The Japanese Union of Scientists and Engineers (JUSE) developed the now widely accepted 14 Points for total quality improvement.

    ☐ a. True

    ☐ b. False

3. Total quality involves:

    ☐ a. Meeting customer needs

    ☐ b. Continuous improvement

    ☐ c. Teamwork

    ☐ d. All of the above

4. Which of the following is not part of the criteria for the Malcolm Baldrige National Quality Award?

    ☐ a. Leadership

    ☐ b. Strategic planning

    ☐ c. Customer satisfaction

    ☐ d. None of the above

NOTES

Unit 2   **TEAMWORK**

This unit has three learning objectives. After completing this unit you will have learned:

1.   What groups are and how groups function.

2.   What the difference is between a group and a team.

3.   What must be done in order to have successful Continuous Improvement Team interaction.

Psychologists have found that most people have strong social and affiliation needs. Because of this it is inevitable that groups of people form and that most people affiliate with one or more groups.

Groups will be found everywhere in our society. People affiliate with churches, civic and fraternal organizations, community action groups, political organizations, hobby clubs, sports organizations, youth groups and every other imaginable type of group. At work the organization as a whole can be considered a group. However, within the organization there are many different types of subgroups like departments, work stations, assembly lines, committees and task teams. Because groups are so much a part of our lives it is unlikely that you can think of anyone you know personally who is not a member of a group of one type or another.

CHARACTERISTICS OF GROUPS

Groups consist of people who possess individual characteristics and traits. However, the group as an entity often takes on characteristics which are quite different from those of the individuals within the group. Here are some of the distinguishing characteristics that groups have:

1.   *Common Purpose:* People tend to form groups when there is a common purpose or objective to be accomplished. An example would be a citizen's action group forming to help protect a neighborhood through a "crime watch" program.

2.   *Common Attitudes:* Members within a group often share a common outlook or have similar interests and values.

3.   *Unity:* Groups can often accomplish far more than individual members by virtue of the strength, unity and cohesiveness of their combined effort.

4. *Social Control:* Groups develop their own codes or norms of social behavior. They establish a broad range of standards from job performance standards and work quotas to rules governing conduct, customs and ritual.

5. *Structure:* Eventually, groups develop their own hierarchy by establishing rank and status within the group.

Another interesting characteristic of groups is that they can be either formal or informal. Formal groups are usually appointed or elected or formed through a consensus (acclamation). Examples of formal groups in business are quality improvement teams, formal work units, budget review committees, safety committees and company credit unions. Formal groups usually have leaders who have been appointed or elected.

Informal groups may take the form of subgroups within formal groups. For example, an informal group can take the form of a small group of four or six employees who always sit together at lunch and play cards or a small group of employees who resist the introduction of new or improved work methods. Also, informal groups usually have leaders. However, the leadership of informal groups is rarely elected or appointed; instead it simply evolves. It is very important to note that for better or worse, informal group leaders can often have more influence on group behavior than formal leaders.

GROUPS VERSUS TEAMS

Groups are not necessarily teams. In fact, there can be a very considerable difference between a team and a group even though groups and teams share certain of the same characteristics. Within both groups and teams can be found common purposes, common attitudes, unity, etc. However, in order for a group to be a team there must be something more than these characteristics.

Members of a team not only have a common purpose but in addition they are mutually committed to achieve a common goal. They fully share information that is relevant about their task or mission with each other in an open, honest and candid way. All of the members of a team actively participate in the team's problem solving efforts to the full limit of their individual and collective capabilities. Team members encourage each another and try to tap the full creative potential of all team members. They have a special sense of team loyalty and cohesiveness. When disagreement or conflict arises they deal with it openly and constructively using problem solving rather than trying to suppress it or compromise. And, team members share responsibility as well as rewards or recognition for their accomplishments.

You might think that the above description also fits practically any group. But this is not the case. A group most definitely does not function as a team if there is unresolved conflict among group members or if some group members withhold relevant problem solving information from the others. The importance of this is that teams are capable of doing something that is impossible for most groups. While it is true that the product of a group can be superior to the product of the average individuals within the group, teams can achieve synergism! Synergism occurs when the product of the team is superior the product of the <u>best</u>, not average, individual on the team. In other words in teams two plus two can equal more than four!

TEAM LEADERSHIP

It is possible for teams to be leaderless. Some organizations are experimenting with what is termed "self-directed teams." These teams often do not have a formally appointed leader. Rather, each member of the team assumes responsibility for providing his or her share of team leadership as the situation requires. In fact, within any effective team, leadership flows among the team members depending on any of several variables. Although self-directed and leaderless teams can serve a useful purpose under certain conditions, experience has proved that Continuous Improvement Teams function most effectively if there is a formally appointed team leader.

The team leader on a CIT has a special role that may be very different from his or her regularly assigned role within the organization -- especially if the team leader also holds a supervisory position. The appointment of a formal team leader does not relieve the team from sharing responsibility. This means that much of the responsibility for ensuring that the team productively focuses on the problem or task, and at the same time maintain effective intra-team interaction, is shared by all of the team members. This helps ensure the quality of the team's problem solving effort and at the same time provides a sense of shared satisfaction for the teams accomplishments among all team members.

An effective team leader is really a coach and a facilitator. The team leader leads through a process of influence that is significantly affected by the extent to which he or she is trusted and accepted by the other members of the team. While trust and acceptance is always important to a leader it is especially important when a leader is not the administrative superior of the team members, as is the case of many Continuous Improvement Teams. In one way, being a CIT team leader is similar to being the leader of a voluntary community action group. The latter has very little position power and, instead must influence group members another way.

The members of a volunteer group can choose to follow or not follow the group leader, something that a subordinate of a supervisor is not free to do. Because the volunteer group leader cannot order or compel members to comply with directions or instructions he or she must find other ways to influence them. There is a high degree of voluntarism within CITs. If someone really does not want to participate in a CIT they are usually free to decline. CIT members participate because they are interested in the nature of their assignment and committed to achieving continuous improvement in costs, quality and productivity. They follow the leadership of the CIT team leader not because they are compelled to do so but rather because they accept that person in a team leadership role.

At the same time, successful CIT team leaders sustain their acceptance by their team members by engaging in a set of behaviors that combines a focus on the accomplishment of their continuous improvement goals with a focus on the needs and goals of the members of the team.

For example, the late Dr. Dennis Kinlaw, an expert in superior team development, found that the most successful team leaders regularly engage in team building practices that focus on:

1. **Action**: The team leader helps the team to get things done, solve problems and overcome organizational obstacles.

2. **Performance**: The team leader is a coach and a facilitator who strives for performance excellence on behalf of the team.

3. **Improvement**: The team leader continuously works with team members to creatively and innovatively identify ways by which improvement can be achieved.

4. **Contact**: The team leader maintains close contact and open communication with employees and key people in other work units.

5. **Relationships**: The team leader ensures that harmonious work relationships are maintained within the team and with others and constructively resolves conflict.

6. **Development**: The team leader places emphasis on developing new skills and competencies both for self and for members of the team.

7. **Team Interaction**: The team leader is a team player who shares responsibility and recognition with other members of the team.

8. **Personal Characteristics**: The team leader sets a personal model of conduct and behavior for other team members to follow.

SUMMARY

Because people have strong social and affiliation needs, groups are inevitable. When groups form they often exhibit characteristics that can be distinguished from the characteristics of the individuals who make up groups. For example, all groups have a *common purpose*, share *common attitudes*, have *unity*, *social control*, and possess a *structure*.

Groups can be either formal or informal. Formal groups are either appointed or elected while informal groups simply evolve within formal groups. However, both informal groups and informal leaders can exert strong influence over other group members and can significantly affect group performance.

Groups are not necessarily teams. Teams are different from groups in that not only do teams have group characteristics but in addition team members share a degree of loyalty, commitment, responsibility and openness that enable them to achieve problem solving synergism. These additional qualities are what makes Continuous Improvement Teams so successful.

Leaders of CITs must function more like a coach and facilitator than like a traditional manager or supervisor. In order to do this the most successful CIT leaders have been found to regularly engage in constructive team building behaviors that focus on Action, Performance, Improvement, Contact, Relationships, Development, Team Interaction and Personal Characteristics of the team leader.

12

TEST & DISCUSSION QUESTIONS

1. Informal groups are usually appointed by higher management.

    ☐ a. True

    ☐ b. False

2. Teams and groups have little in common.

    ☐ a. True

    ☐ b. False

3. Leadership in Continuous Improvement Teams often evolves informally.

    ☐ a. True

    ☐ b. False

4. Successful CIT leaders sustain their acceptance by team members mainly through the process of trust and loyalty.

    ☐ a. True

    ☐ b. False

NOTES

Unit 3   # TEAM DECISION MAKING & PROBLEM SOLVING

This unit has two learning objectives. After completing this unit, you will have learned:

1. Why team decision making and problem solving skills are key to the success of CITs.

2. How to use a 5-step method to make decisions and solve problems.

Importance of Decision Making & Problem Solving

In our everyday life we are put in situations that require us to make decisions and solve problems. The experience of decision making and problem solving is common to all of us. It is also common to CIT programs. The major differences between our personal experience and that of a CIT team with respect to decision making and problem solving are:

1. In our personal lives we tend to make decisions and solve problems alone, not as a part of a group. CIT members usually do this as a team.

2. The subject matter in our personal decision-making and problem-solving efforts is usually different from CIT issues; ours is less work-oriented than the issues that are studied as part of a CIT.

There are many benefits in approaching decision making and problem solving as a team effort. For example, team members can benefit by increasing their understanding of the organization and its employees. Also, they learn that others have problems too, and sharing problems and working toward common solutions can strengthen relations between employees. Having the opportunity to question and offer suggestions facilitates creative thinking. A team atmosphere which promotes participation fosters expression of natural abilities and individual thinking, which are necessary to discover solutions. Participation also helps people to accept changes which may occur. If people take part in decisions about changes, they are often able to adjust more easily to the changes and its future effects.

Often the attention to problem issues and efforts that CIT members expend to solve them results in better quality work. Management also benefits from the information that becomes available to them. With involvement programs, management can receive valuable information from employees who are part of the whole organizational process. Involvement opens up communication between managers and their employees which, in turn, results in the employees supplying information needed problem identification and solution finding.

Decision making and problem solving are very similar in concept and process. The basic difference is that one follows the other. A problem can be described as something that is happening now or has already happened and should be corrected. To correct it, the <u>cause</u> of the problem must be identified. This is called problem solving.

Decision making centers more upon the future. Decisions are made so that future action can be taken. Decision making is the process for choosing *what to do* about the problem. Of course, it is obvious that it is impossible to solve a problem without a decision of some kind being made. But not all decisions solve problems.

The CIT program requires and thrives on team decision making. Team decision making is often the most effective form of decision making when the issues are complex and affect many people or different functions of an organization. While team decision making is usually a slower process than decision making by individuals, it is usually more accurate and does a better job obtaining the commitment of all parties who are affected by the decision.

Depending upon the nature of the team and the problem at hand, the amount of participation within the team may vary. Some members may contribute more than others. But it is still essential that all members participate to the extent that they are able. The roles of management will vary also. There may be certain limits or guidelines the team must work within during the problem-solving and decision-making process. This is reasonable and proper. The role of a team is to support, not supplant, management in its responsibility to effectively manage the affairs of the business or operation.

The Decision Making Process

The decision-making process requires that the team sort out and collect information in a way that problems can be solved. Decision making is most effective when these five steps are followed:

- Identify the problem.

- Gather the facts.

- Develop possible solutions.

- Select the best solution.

- Decide and act.

1.   *Identify the Problem*

This is the first and most important step in the decision-making process. It must first be determined if a problem exists. Once the problem is determined, then it must be located, defined, and limited before any other step can be taken. The solution will not be effective if the problem is not correctly defined.

In order to accurately define the problem it is necessary to determine its extent. Does it occur only in certain departments? When does the problem occur and how often? Once these and other questions are answered, then the problem can be defined. Care must be taken that the problem is not confused with its symptoms. For example, a supervisor discovers that there is too much overtime in his department. Is too much overtime caused by lack of staff, constant breakdowns in equipment, high absenteeism, or poor planning? Any of these factors could be either a cause or a symptom. For example, lack of staff to do the job may be a symptom resulting from the root cause of poor planning the amount of people that are required in the department.

2.   *Gather Facts*

The next step in the process is to examine the problem. After the problem has been defined, the team must gather and evaluate the facts. This includes determining the variance or gap between what has occurred and what was originally planned. The team must look for what was different, what was the condition was that resulted in the change of events that caused the problem.

To do this, you will need both general and detailed facts. If the subject is work quality in a particular department then gather information on quality performance for the organization as a whole as well as specific quality issues and data within the department being studied. The quality of work on certain equipment may be the problem, not the quality of the total department's efforts. Get facts from every possible source. A checklist is a good way to keep a record of the facts. A list is easy to follow and is easy for others to understand. Talk with others in your team and share as much information as possible.

Subjectivity such as prejudice or bias must not affect the evaluation of the facts. The CIT team should study all data openly and objectively. The team should examine every possible cause to see if it produced the change of events, or the problem. The team must also guard against settling for a superficial explanation simply to get an answer to the problem. If poor reasons or explanations are accepted, more problems will occur rather than solving the one at hand.

3.   *Develop Possible Solutions*

The third step in the decision-making process is to develop possible solutions. At this point the team must begin to develop alternative solutions. A very common error is to not consider enough possible solutions. A better decision will result if there are a reasonable number of alternatives to choose from. A decision can only be as good as the "best" of the alternatives. It is also important that the team members remain open-minded and flexible when looking at information. They must not overlook any information that could be important for the solution of the problem and they should be willing to consider and explore all possible solutions.

When evaluating solutions, many factors, such as cost, labor, resources available, effort involved, long-range effects, etc., can be considered in determining which solution is best. For example, if a solution is extremely expensive to the organization, it may not be practical. But if the basic idea can be retained and a less expensive method discovered, then the solution may be very practical. In some cases two or more solutions may seem to be equally feasible. In that event, one or more alternatives might be combined to develop a single "best" solution. The key to this step is the process for developing solutions.

This step of the decision making process highlights team interaction. Each individual is a valuable resource to the team. Someone may examine information about the problem and come up with a certain point of view or a relationship between the facts that was not seen before. Or, he or she may discover a hidden fact overlooked by the others. Members who may have less work experience than others can make significant contributions, also. They may look at the situation with a "fresh eye" because they can stand back and look objectively at a work method, for example, that for them has not yet become a drilled routine. Sometimes we are so close to something we cannot easily be objective about it. How often when we go shopping and tries on an item of clothing do we ask a friend, "How does it looks to you?" Someone who is not wearing the clothing can look at it more objectively.

4.   *Select the Best Solution*

The fourth step in the decision-making process is to select the best solution. In this step the team must assess the various outcomes of each possible solution and evaluate factors such as the cost of implementation, practicability, acceptance by those affected, compatibility with organization policy, and, of course, whether a particular solution will really resolve the problem issue. There are many factors to consider. Advice from others who have confronted similar problems can be valuable additional input, as well. In all instances it is important that the advantages and disadvantages of each alternative solution are clear and that the alternatives are narrowed to a small number of possibilities.

5. *Decide and Act*

This is the last step in the decision-making process. After a final decision has been made, it must be put into action. This includes the determination of the responsibility of the individuals involved, the controls to be used, and the identification of any major difficulties that may occur and how to handle them. The decision is communicated to those affected along with the reasoning behind it, the action to be taken, each person's role, and the expected results. Putting the solution into action is easier when those affected participate in the decision-making process, because then they are more likely to accept the decision. Once the execution of the solution is completed, a follow-up must be made to ensure that the expected results occur and are maintained.

The follow-up of a solution take many forms, depending on all the factors related to it. It may be a short written report evaluating the solution and its effects. Or, with a very complex decision, the follow-up evaluation may be lengthy and detailed. In any case, information must be obtained to measure the effects of the solution. CIT members may be given this responsibility. If so, the follow-up will help the team and management identify the elements that made the decision-making process successful, and these factors can be incorporated in future problem solving efforts. Conversely, the follow-up evaluation will also help to identify the negative factors or weak points in the decision making process so that they can be avoided in the future. If the solution is found to be unsatisfactory, the whole decision-making process should be done again. The entire problem is reviewed and fresh thinking can be applied to finding a sound answer.

SUMMARY

The decision-making process is a basic five-step approach. The process can be very effective in employee involvement programs where a team of people work toward a common goal, to solve a problem. Both the team members and the organization benefit from sharing the responsibilities of this process. Both parties increase their knowledge about the other and relations between employees and management are strengthened.

The problem-solving and decision-making processes are almost identical. However, problem-solving focuses on the past while decision-making is the process for choosing what to do about the problem now or in the future. The five steps for decision-making as it applies to solving problems are:

1. Identify the problem.
2. Gather the facts
3. Develop possible solutions.
4. Select the best solution.
5. Decide and act

Each step of the process requires team members to be open and flexible in order that all information is made available, shared and evaluated. A supportive team atmosphere allows people to think creatively when seeking solutions. The skills in this process can be learned and improved through practice and experience. Members of the team are a valuable resource in the CIT program, and have the opportunity to influence and shape decisions that affect them.

TEST & DISCUSSION QUESTIONS

1. An added benefit that occurs during team problem solving is:

   ☐ a. Relations between employees and management are strengthened.

   ☐ b. Problems are solved quickly.

   ☐ c. Decisions are made solely by management.

   ☐ d. All of the above.

2. The problem solving process is almost identical to the process of:

   ☐ a. Choosing what to do about the problem.

   ☐ b. Making decisions.

   ☐ c. Identifying and understanding the cause of the problem.

   ☐ d. Looking for alternatives.

3. The first and most important step in the decision-making process is:

   ☐ a. Examine the problem.

   ☐ b. Develop possible solutions.

   ☐ c. Identify the problem.

   ☐ d. Gather facts.

4. When developing solutions and selecting the best one, it is important that:

   ☐ a. Things are done as quickly as possible.

   ☐ b. Team members are open-minded and flexible.

   ☐ c. Team members are more concerned about the favorable outcomes.

   ☐ d. Costs are used to judge the results.

NOTES

Unit 4   **TEAM MEETING LEADERSHIP**

This unit has three learning objectives. After completing this unit, you will have learned:

1. How to set up and prepare for a task-oriented conference or meeting.

2. How to avoid common pitfalls that cause meeting ineffectiveness.

3. How to be an effective CIT meeting leader.

Conferences & Meetings

Conferences and meetings are common throughout business, industry and government. Almost all of us attend meetings of one type or another. Weekly staff meetings, briefing meetings, safety or grievance committee meetings, seminars, production meetings, town hall meetings, training sessions, family conferences, student conferences and so very many more types of meetings, large or small, exist that it almost staggers the imagination. At the same time meetings and conferences illustrate how difficult the process of communication can be.

The nature and purpose of meetings may vary but they all share one thing in common. People assemble for the purpose of processing and sharing information. And, yet, so many times this most fundamental purpose is not accomplished because of one main reason, poor conference or meeting leadership. Chief among all other possible causes for conference or meeting failure, poor leadership costs business, industry, government, taxpayers, and private citizens - billions of dollars each year in direct and indirect conference and meeting costs, including preparation, attendance and travel time and cost, facilities and materials cost, and in inefficiencies, lost productivity, lost sales, higher operating costs, lower profits and higher taxes. That is the bad news. The good news is that you can improve your own conference and meeting leadership skills and significantly improve the chances that your conference or meeting will be successful!

Preparing for a Meeting

Most CIT leaders (and often members) are commonly called upon to conduct meetings or conferences. Because of this they should understand the skills required for this function. Preparing for the meeting involves several steps which the meeting leader should carefully follow:

1. **Know your objective**

    Specifically, what do you want to accomplish at your meeting? What can be the best outcome of the meeting? What is the least that can be achieved? Is a meeting really necessary to accomplish your objective? Could you get the desired result in some other way such as an email or telephone call.

2. **Decide who should who attend**

   Meetings are costly. In terms of manpower costs, you can figure the costs by adding the hourly rate of each individual who attends, then multiply that sum by the number of hours the meeting lasts. Also, there may be preparation and other costs. Make sure you have the right people in order to meet your objective.

3. **Schedule the meeting**

   Scheduling your meeting should not simply be a matter of personal convenience. Remember that you do want the right people in attendance. Other people have busy schedules, too. Try to work out a schedule that is most convenient for everyone. Make sure you let your meeting participants know about the meeting.

4. **Prepare an agenda**

   This is the most important part of preparation. An agenda is a list of subjects to be covered in the meeting, in a specific order. It may also include who is to play what role in the meeting and who is to discuss which subject. If your meeting is to be led by one or more team members and you, make sure that all of you prepare your agenda and have a copy of it. The agenda is necessary for the orderly and effective conduct of the meeting.

5. **Arrange the physical setting**

   Often meeting arrangements are not given enough thought and preparation. However, they can have an important impact on the quality and outcome of your meeting. Among the most important meeting arrangements are:

   Comfort - This concerns lighting, heating, ventilation, comfort of seats and similar matters. The comfort should be sufficient so that members can participate without being bothered by excessive heat, noise or the absence of tables upon which they can write and place materials.

   Accessibility - The meeting should be held at a location which most of the participants can conveniently reach. Getting away from the immediate work area (even to another location within the same facility) can help cut down on interruptions. Arrangements should also be made to accommodate participants who may be physically disabled.

Size - This issue is related to the comfort factor. The size of the room should be comfortable for the number of people attending.

Equipment - Paper, pencils or pens, flip charts, felt tip marker, chalkboard and chalk, audio visual equipment (including extension cords and spare bulbs), computers, pointers and telephone are all among the equipment that may be required for your meeting.

Seating - It is known that the seating arrangement of members can affect their participation. It also can determine the amount of control you have in conducting the meeting.

If possible, try to seat participants in a circular or square pattern. Round or square tables are best because they eliminate a formal "head" position and encourage participation. Regardless of the arrangement, try to seat the people with whom you might have difficulty in terms of control immediately to your right of left. This way, by simply leaning forward, you can get the people opposite you more involved in the discussion.

Meeting Leadership

The most successful leaders are those who share responsibilities with the team, maintain team members' satisfaction, and promotes the effectiveness of the team's interaction. The effective leader also adapts his or her manner to the objectives of the meeting and to its expectations. He or she guides the meeting to keep it on course so that it covers what is needed within the allotted period of time. But the leader should remain flexible, since the method of communication may change slightly as the meeting progresses. A key point, for example, may have to be explained more carefully if the leader realizes that some members may not understand it. It is important that the leader and the meeting members give each other feedback so that the objective of the meeting is reached.

The communication process is also important to the role of the leader. It is most effective if all of the members are encouraged to participate in the discussion. This helps keep the atmosphere or emotional climate of the meeting more positive. Keeping the atmosphere relaxed and friendly helps members of the team to more effectively cooperate with each other. A positive atmosphere also encourages other members to assume leadership by taking over part of the discussion initiated by the original leader in which they might have particular knowledge or expertise. As a result, leadership roles can change depending on the topic under discussion and/or the meeting objectives. This is a natural process that shows trust in the "official" team leader and in the entire team so that other team members feel free to express themselves.

Meeting Participation

Meeting members should be expected to fully participate and to contribute to the accomplishment of the meeting's objectives to the extent that their ability will allow. This is very important to the success of the meeting and therefore all members who are participating should encourage the full inclusion of all other meeting members during discussion periods. The role of the participant is to participate; to ask questions, to share information (both facts and ideas), to offer suggestions, to disagree and to criticize constructively, and to encourage his or her fellow members to participate in a like manner. But often it is difficult for those who are in the meeting to objectively and accurately critique the quality of meeting participation. One way to do this is by using a conference participation diagram as shown in Figure 4-1.

Conference Participation Diagram

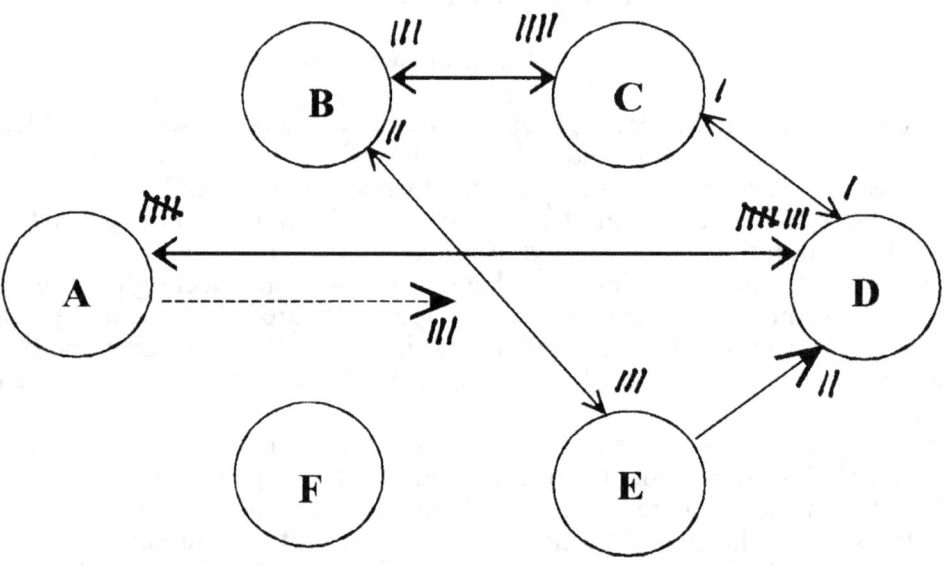

Figure 4-1

A conference participation diagram is a graphic depiction of the communication flow that takes place during a meeting over short periods of time. The diagram is prepared by observers who record the communication flow on flip charts or marker boards at randomly selected "cuts" of the meeting that are usually of five minutes duration each. It is easy to prepare the diagram. In Figure 4-1, circled letters of the alphabet represent meeting participants in the order in which they are seated at a conference table. For the purpose of this illustration **"A"** is designated the meeting leader.

A solid line connecting two participants indicates direct communication from one person to the other. An arrow head shows the direction of communication (from one person to the person at whom the arrow is pointing). Arrow heads at both ends of the solid line indicate that a response was made; i.e., two-way communication. Hash marks next to an arrow head show the frequency of communication from the other party to that person. For example, in Figure 4-1 **"A"** might have said "Thank you **"D"** that is a good idea." That would be a direct communication from **"A"** to **"D"** and would be represented by a solid line between the two with an arrow head at **"D's"** end and one hash marks next to the arrow head. Further, in the diagram it can be seen that **"A"** spoke to **"D"** eight times and that **"D"** responded to **"A"** five times. Lastly, a dotted line to the center of the group represents an indirect communication from one person to the group as a whole. For example, "Well, how should we begin?" In the handout three indirect communications were made by **"A"** to the group in general. The diagram does not distinguish between statements and questions.

Now, refer again to Figure 4-1. In the five minute "cut" recorded by the observer it can be seen that the greatest amount of communication was between **"A"** and **"D."** It is possible that the relatively excessive amount of communication between "A" and "D" stifled more extensive communication among the other members. It is also possible that **"D"** was trying to monopolize the discussion. Meanwhile, **"B"** and **"C"** seem to have engaged in a side conversation. **"D"** and **"C"** exchanged one communication each but **"D"** did not respond to **"E"'s** communication. **"F"** did not participate in the discussion at all. Also, there were three indirect communications from **"A"** to the group in general, and so on.

The conference participation diagram is a very useful tool for assessing the extent of participation of members during a meeting or team discussion. It can be used as often as needed to help meeting participants develop a better process of inclusion among all members. You can easily demonstrate the benefits of this tool by conducting this activity as part of your communication skills training program and by encouraging the class to use the process whenever they want to critique the quality of the meetings that they attend.

Hidden Agenda

A dysfunctional occurrence in some meetings is when one or more members have a *hidden agenda.* We have referred to the term "agenda" in meeting preparation as being a plan, a list of subjects to be covered in a specific order. The term is used here in reference to a plan or motive that is not seen, not revealed by the member. It is a personal plan, a hidden plan held by a team member. It consists of attitudes and desires, motives and emotional reactions which cannot be fitted openly into the team task.

This barrier to communication can often be seen during the opening of a meeting when individual puts out "feelers" to probe the attitudes of others. The meeting participant wants to know what is expected and how his or her contribution will fit into the team, who has and will have power, who will compete against him or her and who will be a friendly ally. Both members and leaders may have hidden agendas. During this probing period, a person will often cautiously frame his or her questions and answers according to what the "feelers" find. The leader should be sensitive to these hidden agendas and recognize what a team can or cannot talk about at a given time. The leader should strive for openness and let the team know that he or she is aware of individual differences and feelings and that they can be used creatively and constructively. By reducing hidden agendas the team can more easily accomplish its task.

Conflict

Conflict has a direct relationship to the maturity and candor of a team. How it is handled will determine the team atmosphere. Conflict can be either positive or negative depending upon the commitment the team has in reaching its objective. Conflict can be task-centered; caused by time pressure, lack of proper equipment, lack of information about the problem, etc. Or it can be people-centered; caused when the needs of members are unfulfilled; i.e., the need to belong, control, self-interest or the need for acceptance. Conflict can be handled most effectively by trying to resolve the problem when it arises. All members should be heard and given fair consideration, and members should not take a "win or lose" attitude. Differences of opinion will naturally occur and they should be thoroughly discussed.

As indicated earlier, conflict is not inherently dysfunctional. The basic nature of conflict is simply disagreement - not open warfare. Conflict can have a positive affect on the meeting because the different ideas that are presented can offer a deeper understanding of the topic or problem. This makes solution-finding smoother and, in turn, can stimulate and motivate the team members.

Meeting Leader Functions

There are several critical functions that are required of any meeting leader. These are things that must be done in order to accomplish the objectives of the meeting. They are of two types: The first is *task functions* - those required to get the job done.

Introducing - getting started, discussing the objectives.

Clarifying - making sure statements are understood.

Summarizing - reviewing issues.

Agreement Checking - to determine what level of agreement exists among team members.

The second type, *team relations* functions, are those which are necessary to maintain smooth and cooperative relationships among meeting members.

Encouraging - helping others to express themselves.

Expressing Feelings - being sensitive to the team's emotions.

Harmonizing - keeping conflict from creating serious problems.

Modifying - being willing to change one's position when the facts require it.

Gate Keeping - maintaining open communication.

Evaluating - determining how well members are interacting and making progress on the team task.

Conducting an Effective Meeting

Now, let us put all of this together into 10 tips which will help you be more effective when you conduct your next meeting:

1. Begin your next meeting by clearly stating the purpose and objective that you want to have accomplished.

2. Review the meeting agenda. Briefly discuss any details or ground rules concerning the meeting; e.g., length of meeting, co-leader, reference material, etc.

3. Encourage participants to share their views about the subject and objective of the meeting together with any related information that they have not yet shared.

4. State your own views and then suggest an explanation of the issue or problem to be solved.

5. Discuss what process will be most suitable for dealing with the problem.

6. Encourage suggestions, ideas and other inputs from participants. Be sure to employ the team relations functions described earlier.

7. When alternatives have been fully explored or a solution is found for the problem, or new ideas have been added, make a summary of where the team stands.

8. Check the level of agreement of team members when the decision or solution is found.

9. Decide on any follow-up action, set follow-up dates and assign responsibilities.

10. Get final feedback and then end the meeting.

Summary

Meetings in business, industry, government and in our private lives are a fact of life. Meetings serve an essential purpose; they are one of the most common ways to share and process information among teams of people. However, in many cases, meetings are not effective and result in large wastes of time and money. Chief among the causes of meeting failure is poor meeting leadership. However, meeting leadership skills can be improved with proper commitment and effort.

There are several key steps involved in enhancing meeting leadership skills. The first is to make sure that you have properly prepared for your meeting. The most important steps that should be taken to prepare for the meeting are to determine the meeting objective, decide who should attend, schedule the meeting, prepare an agenda, and arrange the meeting room.

Next, you should understand both your own role as a meeting leader, which is to facilitate or guide and encourage participation, as well as the roles of the individual team members. Following this, you should understand the leader task functions and the team relations functions and apply them to your objective.

TEST & DISCUSSION QUESTIONS

1. The one thing all conferences and meetings have in common is:

   ☐ a. Information sharing and processing.

   ☐ b. Size.

   ☐ c. Good leadership.

   ☐ d. All of the above.

2. Which of the following meeting preparation steps is the most important?

   ☐ a. Knowing your objective.

   ☐ b. Deciding who will attend.

   ☐ c. Preparing an agenda.

   ☐ d. Scheduling the meeting.

3. Which of the following is a role of a meeting leader?

   ☐ a. Sharing responsibilities with the group.

   ☐ b. Adapting his or her manner to the objective of the meeting.

   ☐ c. Keeping the atmosphere relaxed and friendly.

   ☐ d. All of the above.

4. Which of the following is a major role of a meeting participant?

   ☐ a. To guide group discussion.

   ☐ b. To develop hidden agendas.

   ☐ c. To share information.

   ☐ d. To share responsibilities with the group.

NOTES

Unit 5   DATA COLLECTION - CHARTS & GRAPHS

This unit has three learning objectives. After you have completed this unit, you will have learned:

1. Why data collection is important and how it is used in problem solving.

2. How to use sampling techniques to make predictions about the whole lot.

3. How to use charts and graphs to depict data collection results.

Collecting Data

Data is information. Information is needed in order for anyone to solve a problem. Imagine trying to solve a problem without having the necessary information. Problem solving in such a situation would be nothing more than guess work. On the other hand, we seldom have all of the information about a problem that we would like to have. The key is to gather all of the essential information that is available, analyze it and then make a decision based upon the best information that can be developed.

This is why data collection is so important. Data collection will enable you to develop as large an essential information base as possible. When this is done you substantially improve your chances of making an accurate analysis of a problem and of selecting the best solution for it.

There are two kinds of data, facts and perceptions. If relevant to the problem that you are trying to solve, both facts and perceptions should be studied. However, it is very important to distinguish between a fact and a perception. A fact is a truth. It can always be supported by empirical evidence. Perceptions, on the other hand, are beliefs, attitudes or opinions; the way people look at things. The recorded number of customer complaints about late deliveries in a given month is a fact. But, until proven through analysis and study, the reason why deliveries are late is a perception; i.e., a belief or an opinion.

There are several ways by which information can be collected. Perceptual information is usually collected through the use of survey questionnaires and personal interviews. For example, the Total Quality Management Survey that many organizations use in the planning and assessment part of a CIT program is a survey questionnaire that obtains perceptions from employees about total quality conditions within their work unit and within the organization as a whole. In many cases personal interviews are also conducted with employees to validate the results of survey findings and/or to obtain additional information about employees' attitudes, opinions and beliefs regarding total quality issues.

33

Factual information can also be obtained from questionnaires. Information about a person's education, work experience and job knowledge, for example, can be obtained through the use of questionnaires and tests. Factual information can also be collected through observation, instrument measurement and through the process of sampling.

Sampling Methods

Sampling is a method of collecting information about the whole by studying the characteristics, properties and attributes of a statistically selected sampling of the whole. Suppose that your job is to ensure that a lot (a group or batch produced under the same conditions; e.g., by the same person or by the same machine) of 500 small electric motors meets specified quality standards. What do you do?

You could inspect and test each one of the 500 motors. That would enable you to determine with 100% accuracy whether or not the lot met the quality standard. Of course, this would take considerable time and effort which for most organizations would not be cost effective. A more efficient and effective way to do this would be to take a sample of the lot. The sample would be carefully inspected and tested. Data from this procedure would then be used to make a prediction about the entire lot of 500 motors.

Statistical studies have shown that if the proper techniques are used, sampling can be a highly accurate way to determine the characteristics, properties and other aspects of a whole lot. In most cases a small, careful sampling will enable you to make remarkably accurate predictions about the whole. Television pollsters, for example, may take a random sample of only 1,000 to 1,500 from a viewing audience of several million. Yet, it has been proven that a sample of this size can achieve an accuracy of up to 96%.

There are three types of sampling techniques that are commonly used. These are random sampling, systematic sampling and stratified sampling.

> *Random Sampling* is a technique in which samples must be selected from all parts of the lot at random. Each unit in the lot must have an equal chance of being selected.

> *Systematic Sampling* is frequently used to select samples from a continuous production line such as when components move along a conveyor system. In this technique samples are selected at set intervals like one of every 15 units.

> *Stratified Sampling* involves the use of either random sampling or systematic sampling, or both, in order to obtain an accurate cross-section of different machines, shifts, operators, etc.

All three of these techniques require that you adhere to the following steps in order to achieve a proper sampling:

1. Determine the facts that you will need together with the probable sources of those facts. In the majority of sampling situations you will be dealing with physical objects such as lots of material, parts, reports, forms, batches, etc. You must first determine exactly what you need to know about these objects

2. Determine the size of the lot from which you want to take samples. When performing calculations in connection with sampling, lot size is usually indicated by the symbol "N."

3. Determine the size of the sample (indicated by the symbol "n"). There are many guidelines available in the form of sampling tables that will suggest what size sample you will need for any given lot.

4. Determine the format that you will use to record the data. In many cases a simple checklist or tally sheet will be sufficient for this purpose.

5. Select the sampling technique: random, systematic or stratified.

6. Take the sample according to the technique that you have selected.

7. Examine the sample and record your findings.

8. Make a prediction about the entire lot based upon the findings of your sampling.

Here is an example of how sampling works:

Assume that you are dealing with a lot of 500 plastic surgical devices (N=500). Also assume that the sampling table you checked recommends that when N=500 you should take a sample of 8%. In this case n will equal 40 (500 X 8%). If our inspection and testing of the sampling of 40 shows that two or 5% were defective then we can conclude through prediction that 5% of the entire lot, 25, will be defective. We can then compare this rate with whatever the quality standard may be for this particular item.

Displaying Data

Collecting the required data is only one step in the process of data collection and analysis. Once data has been collected, it must be displayed in a manner that will enable you to analyze it. This is usually done by plotting data on charts and graphs. There are many types of charts and graphs that are useful when displaying data. In this unit you will learn how to use four of the more common charts and graphs:

- Bar Charts
- Line Graphs

- Pie Charts
- Scattergrams

Bar Charts are usually used to show a comparison of data. Figure 5-1 illustrates a typical bar chart in which the number of customer complaints is compared over four calendar quarters among four sales districts. When you construct a bar chart be sure to record or list quantities produced or quality levels on the Y Axis, the vertical axis on the left side of the chart. The X Axis, the horizontal line at the bottom of the chart, usually lists information such as time, duration, operator numbers, machine numbers and shifts.

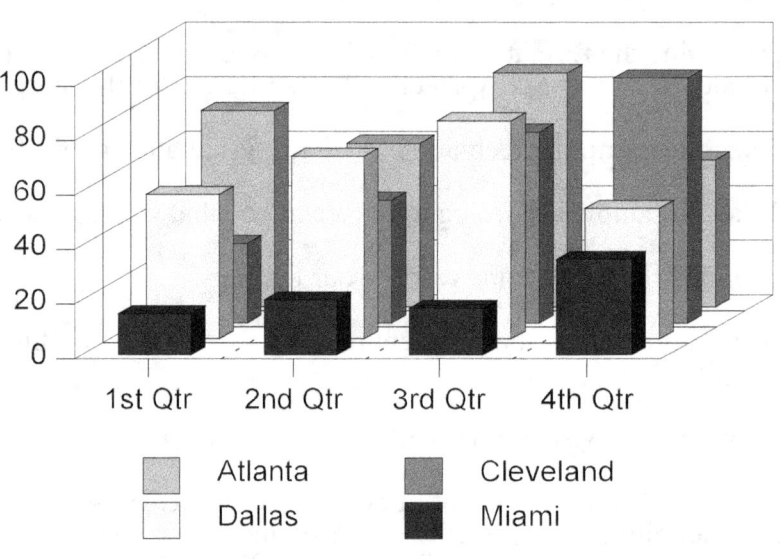

Figure 5-1

(Later you will learn how bar charts are used to plot information developed from Pareto Analysis and in Histograms.)

Line Graphs can sometimes be used to show trends and patterns more effectively than bar charts. A line graph depicts the same kind of data that is listed in bar charts. However, instead of using a bar to show a comparison of data, points are plotted to correspond with the data and lines are then used to connect the points. Figure 5-2 is a line graph that depicts daily production at various work stations. Another useful application of line graphs is in connection with the use of control charts. A control chart is used to signal when a product or component that is being produced, or a service level that is being provided, begins to vary from established quality or quantity standards.

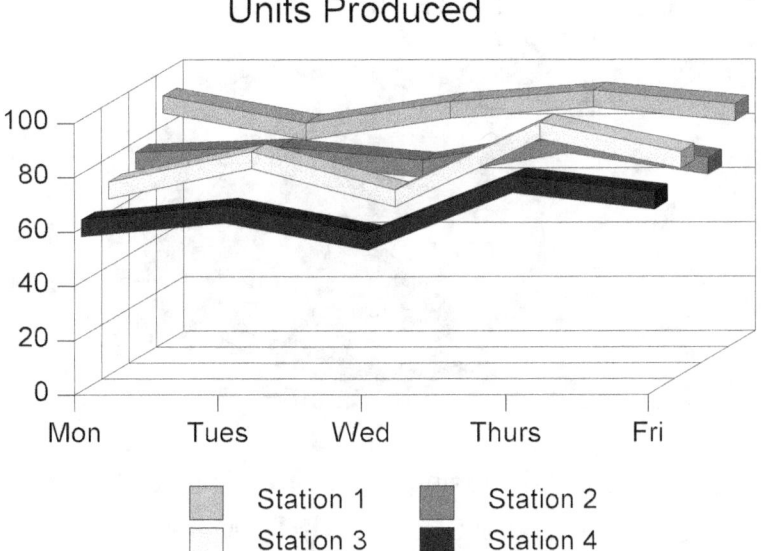

Figure 5-2

Pie Charts are so called because of their circular shape and because their sections resemble the slices of a pie. Pie charts are especially useful for dramatizing the relationship between one component and another. Figure 5-3 shows a pie chart depicting the relationship and magnitude of costs for a marketing project.

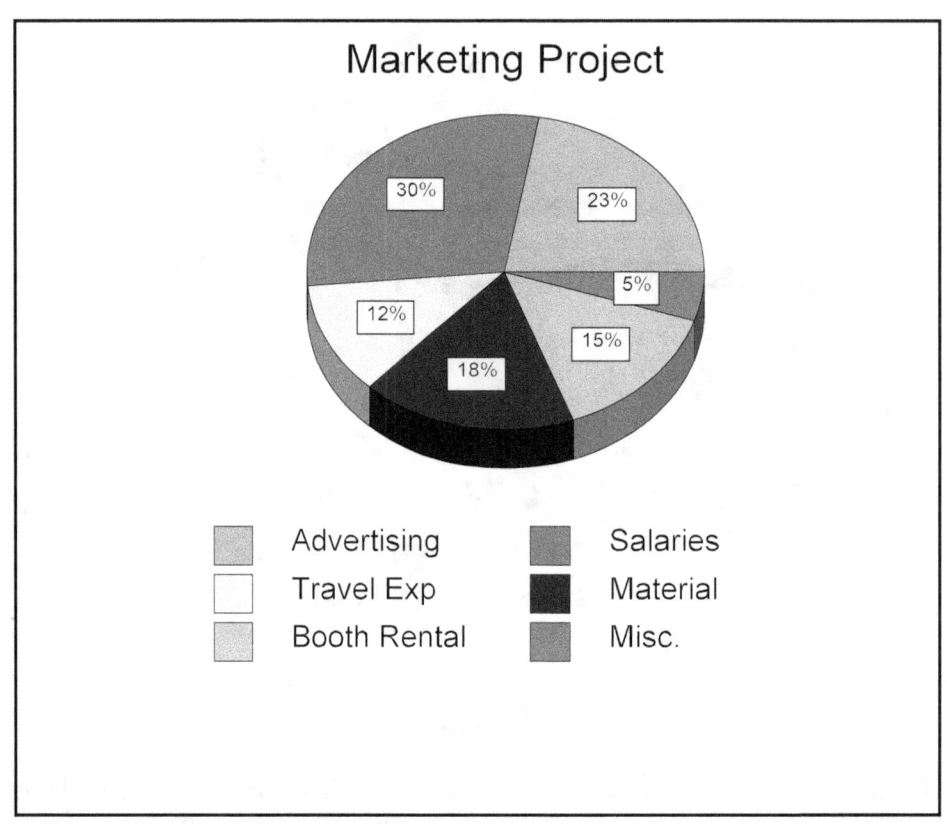

Marketing Project

30%   23%
12%   5%
      15%
   18%

Advertising   Salaries
Travel Exp   Material
Booth Rental   Misc.

Figure 5-3

Scattergrams are perhaps the most unusual of the four types of charts and graphs discussed in this unit. Scattergrams take the form of points which are used to plot the distribution and frequency of data. The points are contained within an X and a Y axis that list the type of information previously cited. In order to understand scattergrams, better suppose that you were collecting data about weight distribution in relation to length of a part. You could simply list this information in tabular form much like writing down a column of numbers. However, it would be much easier to analyze the data if you constructed a scattergram like the one shown in Figure 5-4.

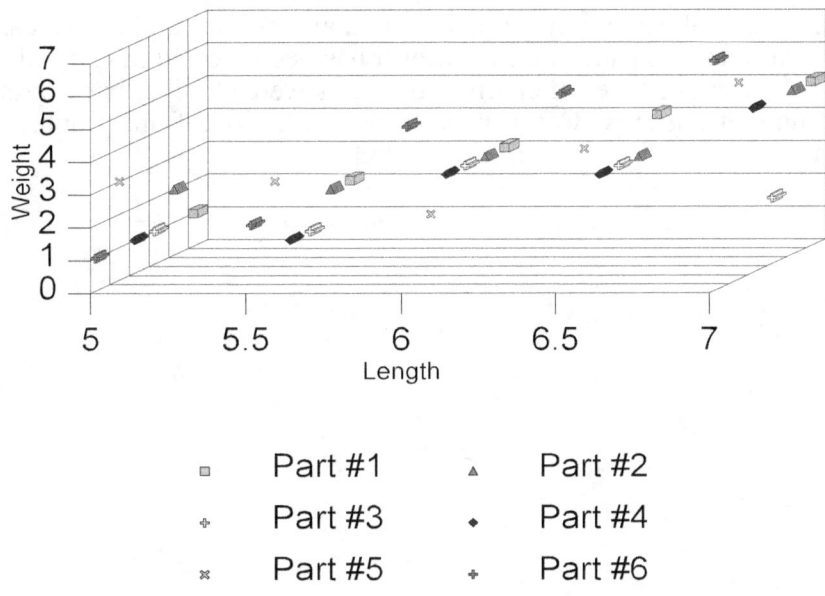

Weight Distribution

Figure 5-4

Scatter grams are also very useful for showing the relationship of two items such as height in relation to weight, costs in relation to units sold and defects in relation to machine speed.

Summary

Data collection is the foundation of accurate problem analysis because a problem cannot be accurately studied and solved unless sufficient reliable information about it is made available. Data takes the form of facts and perceptions. Facts are truths which can be observed, measured and otherwise determined by empirical means. Perceptions are usually attitudes, opinions and beliefs, which by their nature are more subjective.

Data about both facts and perceptions can be collected by using a variety of methods. Observation, measurement with instruments, the use of survey questionnaires, and personal interviews are among the many data collection methods. Still another data collection method is sampling.

Sampling enables you to study the characteristics, properties and other aspects of a whole lot by taking a statistical sample and then submitting the samples to tests and inspection. Based on the results of the testing and inspection of the sample, predictions can be made about the whole lot.

Once data are collected, it must be recorded and analyzed. In most cases it is easier and more effective to analyze data after it has been plotted in chart or graph form. In this unit four major types of charts and graphs were studied: bar charts, line graphs, pie charts and scattergrams. Control charts, as a variation of line graphs, were also studied.

TEST & DISCUSSION QUESTIONS

1. When solving most operational problems you will be collecting data about:

   ☐ a. Facts

   ☐ b. Opinions

   ☐ c. Perceptions

   ☐ d. All of the above

2. The first step of the process that you should use to achieve a proper sampling is to:

   ☐ a. Determine the sample size.

   ☐ b. Decide what facts are needed.

   ☐ c. Select the sampling method.

   ☐ d. Make a prediction.

3. Bar charts are the best for signaling when a control limit is being exceeded.

   ☐ a. True

   ☐ b. False

4. Which of the following charts or graphs is best for dramatizing the relationship of the costs of a component?

   ☐ a. Pie charts

   ☐ b. Scatter grams

   ☐ c. Bar charts

   ☐ d. Line graphs

41

NOTES

Unit 6   PARETO ANALYSIS & HISTOGRAMS

This unit has three learning objectives. After you have completed this unit, you will have learned:

1. What Pareto Analysis is.

2. How to prepare a Pareto distribution.

3. What histograms are and how to construct one.

4. How to use Pareto Analysis and histograms to help quantify data, make comparisons of data and prioritize problem issues.

In the late 1800's an Italian economist, Alfredo Pareto, discovered a remarkable natural phenomenon. Pareto observed that in financial matters 80% of outcomes resulted from only 20% of the causes. For example, 20% of a person's investment portfolio usually produced 80% of the profits.

Remarkably, this observation holds true for things in nature, also. If you cut a tree down and look at the cross-section you have just cut you see the tree's growth rings. Study the stump carefully and you will observe 80% of the rings are contained in 20% of the area of the cross-section. Within the universe 80% of a galaxy's stars can be found in 20% of the space that the galaxy occupies. The chambers of the Nautilus, a crustacean, follow this interesting ratio as do parts and components of almost all matter.

No one knows what the significance of this natural law is. We do know that it exists throughout all of nature and that it affects us in many ways. For example, here are some "80% - 20%" observations about people and things that seem to regularly occur in the work place:

- 80% of all absenteeism and accidents can usually be traced to 20% of the employees.

- 80% of machine downtime is usually caused by 20% of the machines.

- 80% of a company's profits usually comes from 20% of its product line.

- 80% of costs involved in producing a product or service can usually be traced to only 20% of the cost elements.

This ratio exists <u>before</u> any attempt is made to change a condition where the 80/20 rule can be found. After change is made this ratio no longer holds constant.

This interesting phenomenon has important implications for a CIT. program. For example, suppose there is a quality problem concerning the production of defective parts. If we know that 80% of defective work can probably be traced to only 20% of the work stations, we can analyze what is occurring at those stations very carefully. If the conditions causing defects at those work stations are corrected, we will achieve a dramatic improvement in overall product quality!

Pareto Distribution

The most common way to use the Pareto principle is to construct a Pareto chart or graph and analyze the data that it presents. Figure 6-1 shows a Pareto distribution based on a summary of packing errors. Note that five or 20% of the 25 packers in this study account for almost 80% (78.91%) of errors. Any improvement effort will be most successful if it focuses on those packers with the greatest number of errors.

Rank	Packer#	Avg. Nr. Errors	% of Total
1	0054	38.66	27.68
2	0011	27.65	47.50
3	0146	20.58	62.24
4	0130	17.15	74.54
5	0066	6.13	78.91
6	0118	5.84	88.09
7	0085	4.82	86.54
8	0006	4.46	89.78

(Continuation)

Rank	Packer#	Avg. Nr. Errors	% of Total
23	0062	.10	99.89
24	0005	.09	99.96
25	1176	.06	100.00
		140.00	

Figure 6-1

44

The Pareto distribution in Figure 6-1 was made by ranking all 25 packers according to the number of errors they made over a given period of time. From this distribution it can be seen that there was a total of 140 errors for the period. Together the first five ranked packers accounted for 110 of the 140 total errors. Packer # 0054 alone accounted for 38.66 or 27.68% of the total.

We do not know why those particular packers made so many errors. Pareto analysis only shows patterns and trends. Perhaps those packers were among the most recent hires or perhaps they had been given less training than others. Perhaps there is a problem with supervision. Certainly it is important that management promptly investigate the problem further. This will now be much easier to do since the problem has been isolated to only several packers and not to the entire work crew.

Pareto distributions are often combined with other graphic forms for optimum analysis. In the case of packer # 0054 additional study centered on the number of errors that the packer made each week in the month of September. First, a simple tally was made through observation by the supervisor. Figure 6-2 shows how this was done.

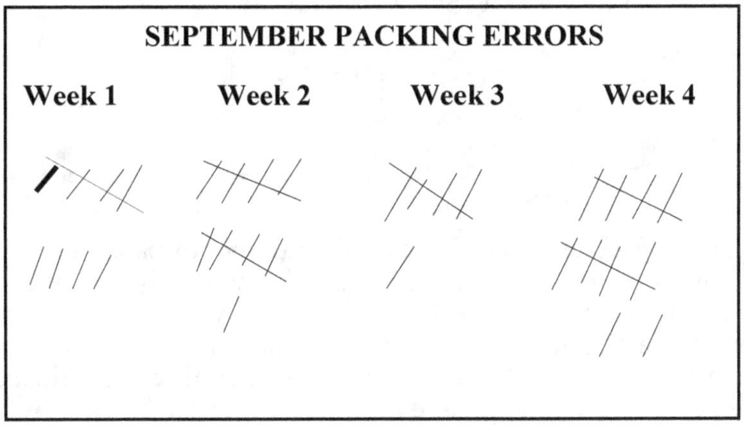

Figure 6-2

In order for the data in the tally sheet to be fully useful it was transferred to a bar graph as in Figure 6-3.

September Packing Errors

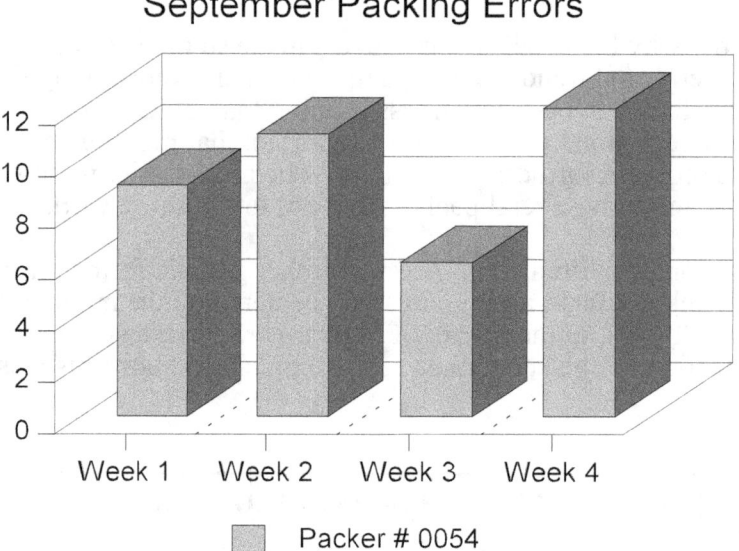

Figure 6-3

Note that with the exception of Week 3 the number of packing errors by packer 0054 increased during the month of September. This would be of concern to the supervisor of the packer and something that he or she would want to study further. The collection and plotting of data about the errors will aid the supervisor to examine the problem in an objective manner. It will also help to avoid a conflict over the actual number of errors when the supervisor discusses the problem with the employee.

When data about only a few items are collected the trend or pattern might be so obvious that charting is not necessary. However, in most situations the amount of data is large enough that charting become essential.

Histogram

The bar graph in Figure 6-3 is also called a histogram. Histograms are charts that are used to compare data over different time periods. As a further example of a histogram, suppose that management in a bank wants to analyze customer complaints about statement errors. If the data were shown month by month over a twelve-month period, it might look like the histogram in Figure 6-4.

Statement Errors

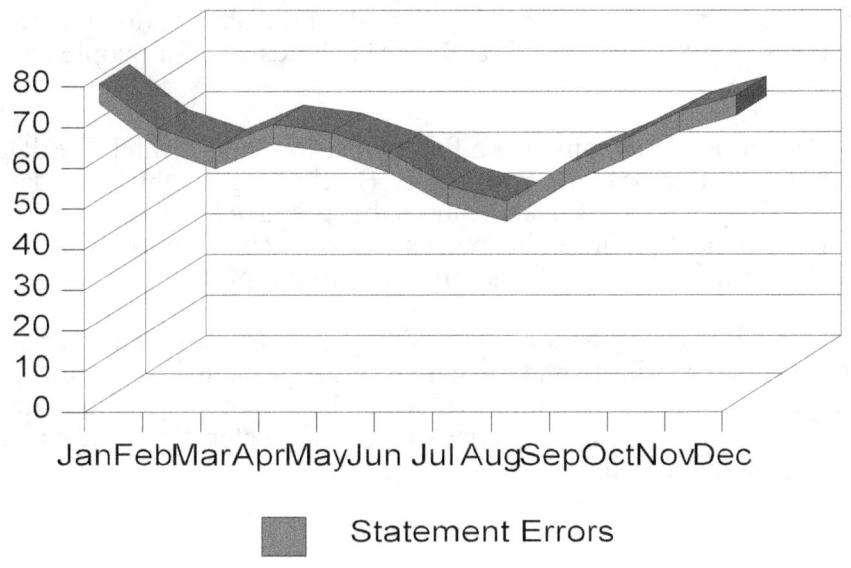

Figure 6-4

The line graph histogram in Figure 6-4 shows an interesting cyclical pattern of customer complaints. It does not show the type of complaint (although it would be possible to construct one that does) nor does it indicate why the complaints occurred. However, the histogram very clearly shows that complaints are lower in the summer months and around the late winter holiday season than at other times of the year. Armed with the knowledge that a pattern of complaints exists, management can now study the problem in greater detail to identify possible causes and to develop alternative solutions.

There are many other examples of how histograms can be used in business and industry to compare data for decision analysis. Some of the uses that organizations have made of histograms range from plotting the life span of light bulbs and determining high and low periods of production efficiency to comparing sales histories between sales territories and analyzing patient census in hospitals.

47

Summary

Often, solving problems can be made easier if the problem can be depicted graphically. One way to do this is by taking advantage of a natural phenomenon called Pareto analysis or the 80/20 rule. This principle is based on the observation that in most cases 80% of outcomes result from 20% of causes. This holds true for people and things alike.

You can use this principle to construct a Pareto distribution in which the data that you want to study is ranked in order of magnitude. By charting or tabulating data in this way you can easily identify the 20% of causes that produce 80% of the results. In a continuous improvement program this means that you can more easily analyze problems such as errors, waste, defects and other similar problems.

Another useful problem analysis tool is the histogram. While Pareto charts plot data according to rank order, priority and the nature of the problem, histograms plot data according to periods of time. Optimum value can be obtained by using both Pareto charts, histograms and other forms of charts to gain a greater degree of understanding about the nature of operational problems.

TEST & DISCUSSION QUESTIONS

1. Pareto analysis is a useful tool but is limited in application since it only applies to "thing" problems.

    ☐ a.   True

    ☐ b.   False

2. Which of the following is the issue that you should first consider when constructing a Pareto chart?

    ☐ a.   The time period desired.

    ☐ b.   The data collection method.

    ☐ c.   What data is required.

    ☐ d.   The kind of chart to use.

3. Histograms usually depict data according to:

    ☐ a.   Rank order.

    ☐ b.   Nature of the problem.

    ☐ c.   Problem severity.

    ☐ d.   Periods of time.

4. In order to avoid confusion Pareto charts and histograms should not be used together to analyze a problem.

    ☐ a.   True

    ☐ b.   False

NOTES

UNIT 7   CAUSE - EFFECT ANALYSIS

This unit has two learning objectives. After you have completed this unit you will have learned:

1. What a cause-effect diagram is and how to construct one.

2. How to use cause-effect analysis to identify problem root causes.

Logically, there is a cause for every problem. In order to effectively solve a problem you must identify what causes it and then remove, eliminate, or correct the cause. It is often very difficult to accurately determine the problem root cause. If you are not successful in identifying the root cause of the problem you might treat only its symptoms - thus, you may never really solve the problem.

This is a very common situation among people who have not received training in problem-solving techniques. Many of us are so eager to solve persistent problems that we tend to latch on to the most visible signs of the problem and assume that we have found the reason why the problem exists. For example, suppose a first level super-visor noticed that the work performance of one of her employees began dropping off after she reassigned him to a different job - a job that the employee had performed quite some time ago. The supervisor may have assumed that because the employee did the job before, he should be able to do it again. The supervisor then calls the employee into her office and ask why his performance seems to be dropping. The employee responds that he feels that since the "new" job is more difficult it should command a higher rate of pay.

It would be easy to conclude that the cause of the employee's poor work performance is dissatisfaction with the pay level. If, as is usually the case for first level supervision, control over pay levels is not within the scope of her responsibility, the supervisor might conclude that there is nothing that she can do about the employee's complaint. In that event poor performance would probably continue until she took some other action like disciplining the employee or transferring him to another job. In fact, in this case, pay had absolutely nothing to do with the reason why the employee's job performance was falling. Discontent with pay was only a symptom of the problem. A more thorough analysis of the problem would have shown that the root cause was that it had been a considerable time since the employee worked on the job to which he was reassigned. The employee needed retraining on the "new" job. In the absence of retraining the job seemed far more difficult than it really was. Why didn't the employee simply indicate this? Perhaps the reason was pride. Perhaps because he did not recognize that retraining was necessary. In any event, it is clear that the supervisor and the employee would have benefitted if she knew how to more accurately determine the problem root cause.

Cause-effect analysis is a method by which you can easily and accurately analyze a problem to determine its root cause. At the same time cause-effect analysis also develops data which will help you to develop alternative solutions to the problem that you have analyzed. The basis of cause-effect analysis is the cause-effect diagram (also know as the "fishbone diagram" and the "Ishikawa Diagram") that was first proposed by Japanese quality expert Kaora Ishikawa. Figure 7-1 shows a basic cause-effect diagram.

Cause-Effect Diagram

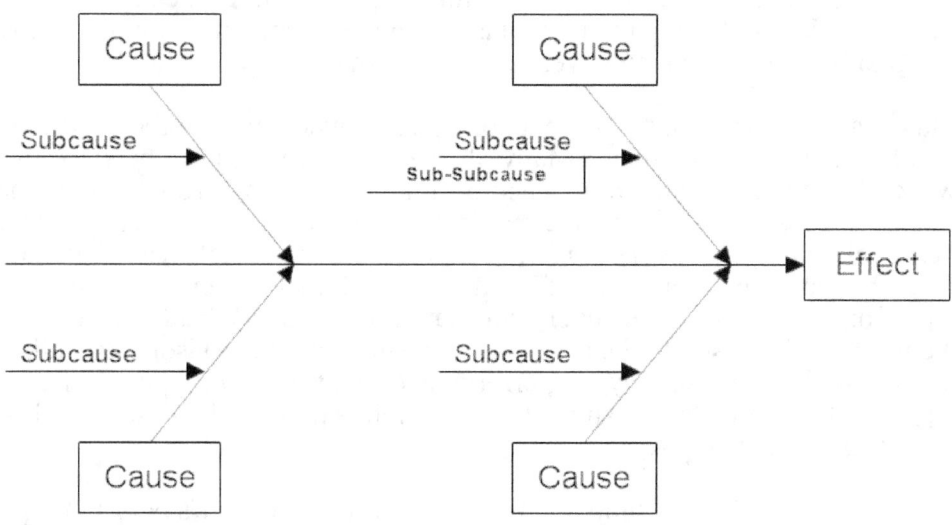

Figure 7-1

The "EFFECT" in Figure 7-1 is the problem that you are trying to solve. The "CAUSE" is the reason why the problem exists. The subcause is the reason why each cause exists and the sub-subcause is the reason why each subcause exists.

When you use cause-effect analysis, you are using the "why" technique - always questioning "why" to the previous step until there are no more plausible answers. At that point you have probably reached the root cause.

Let us further clarify cause-effect analysis by using somewhat more detailed examples such as the one depicted in Figure 7-2.

Cause-Effect Analysis for Chipped Widgets

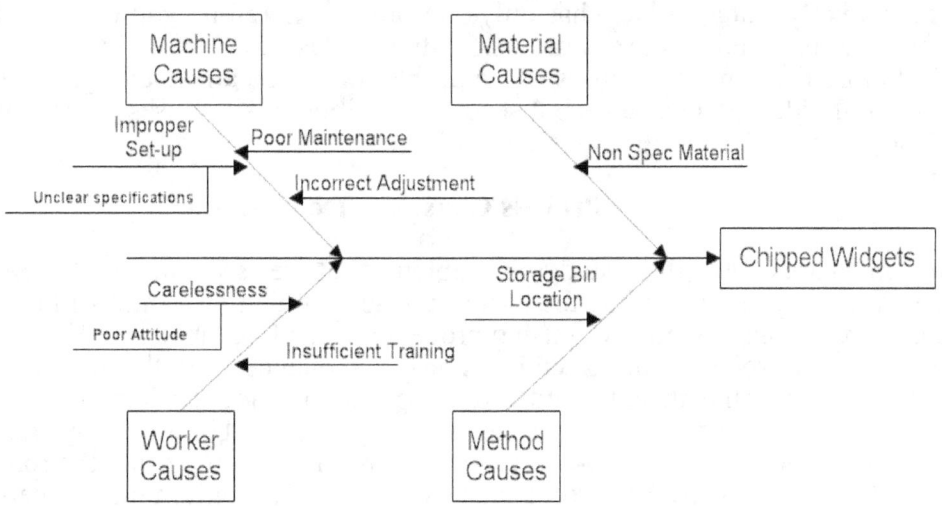

Figure 7-2

In figure 7-2 the basic problem is chipped widgets. This is written in the "EFFECT" space. It is important that you be as precise as possible at this point. The word "scrap," for example, would be far too broad. The kind of scrap in particular would be much more appropriate.

Next, the major causes or reasons why chipped widgets exist are listed. This is done by asking the question "Why are there chipped widgets?" The answer is because of (1) *machine* causes, (2) *material* causes, (3) *method* causes, or (4) *worker* causes. In most cases these four major causes: machines, material, method and worker will apply. You can, of course, use whatever major causes you believe fit the particular problem that you have selected.

The next step is to take each major cause individually and again use the "why" technique. Referring to one of the four major causes, machines, for example, ask "why are there machine problems?" The answer (subcause) might be because of (1) improper set-up, (2) incorrect adjustment, and (3) poor maintenance. Taking this process still one step further, we can now determine subcauses, if any, by again using the "why" technique. Using improper set-up as another example, you can see that unclear specifications was a sub-subcause. Also note that carelessness was a subcause of the worker cause and that the root cause of it was stated as poor attitude. However, if the person making the diagram continues to use the "why" technique then the obvious next question would be "why" does the worker have a poor attitude? This

53

illustrates the need to continue the analysis until the true root cause is found. Correct each sub-cause and eventually the CAUSE will be corrected, thus solving the problem.

It is unlikely that a problem has only one cause. Therefore, you will benefit by constructing as complete a cause-effect diagram as possible. In many cases you will find more than one root causes to the problem that you are studying. Alternatively, you might identify one cause but several contributing subcauses all of which must be remedied in order to fully solve the problem.

Process Cause - Effect Analysis

In some cases you will be studying problems that are associated with steps of an operation or process. While the basic cause-effect diagram could still be used in such cases, you might benefit from using process cause-effect analysis. Each step of the operation or process is indicated in its proper sequence up to the point of the problem (EFFECT) which is then defined. At this point you should select one step at a time to study, usually beginning with the step nearest problem. Use the "why" technique to determine major causes, sub-causes and so on. If you cannot find the root cause in that step then work backwards taking each step and analyzing it in turn. Keep alert for contributing causes that need correction, also.

SUMMARY

One of the most difficult tasks to accomplish when solving a problem is to determine the problem root cause. Failure to do so usually results in treating symptoms of the problem rather than the real reason why the problem exists.

One method for accurately determining problem root causes is to conduct cause-effect analysis using a cause-effect diagram. Here the "effect" is the clearly defined problem while a "cause" is a reason why the problem exists. Cause-effect diagrams consist of major causes, subcauses and sub-subcauses. Each of these is arrived at by using the "why" technique, e.g., "why does the problem exist?" When you reach the point that there are no further answers to the question "why" then you usually have identified the problem root cause.

A companion to basic cause-effect analysis is process cause-effect analysis. This technique is especially helpful for processes or operations which occur in a given sequence. Together, both techniques will help you to substantially improve the quality of your problem diagnosis.

TEST AND DISCUSSION QUESTIONS

1. In order to effectively solve a problem you must first identify its _____.

    ☐ a. Symptoms.

    ☐ b. Apparent cause.

    ☐ c. History.

    ☐ d. Root cause.

2. In cause-effect analysis which of the following represents the specific problem that you are studying?

    ☐ a. Cause.

    ☐ b. Effect.

    ☐ c. Subcause.

    ☐ d. Sub-subcause.

3. In most cases the cause-effect diagram will help you to pinpoint the sole cause of the problem.

    ☐ a. True.

    ☐ b. False.

4. In process cause-effect analysis you should first _____.

    ☐ a. Select one step to study.

    ☐ b. Use the "why" technique.

    ☐ c. List the process or operation in sequence.

    ☐ d. Develop major cause categories.

NOTES

Unit 8   **THE CREATIVE PROCESS**

This unit has three learning objectives. After completing this unit, you will have learned:

1.   What creativity is and what its characteristics are.

2.   How you can identify and remove blocks that hinder full use of the imagination.

3.   How you can improve your potential for creative thinking.

The Nature of Creativity

We all have the capacity for creative thinking, but we don't always utilize it. This is due to a variety of cultural factors stemming from childhood. As we slowly mature, we are directed away from "childish" thinking like spontaneity, wishfulness, openness of mind, and fantasizing. We usually are criticized or ridiculed when we lapse back into this type of behavior. In turn, we become critical of others' ideas and of our own when they seem to extend "out-of-the-box." We discourage speculation. Also, being creative is being risky. If our ideas are accepted, we feel accepted but if our ideas fail, then we believe that we've failed.

To become more creative is not just to learn, but to *unlearn*. It means getting rid of traditional thought patterns, mental and emotional blocks and anti-creative behavior toward others. It also means adopting creative behavior, the characteristics often found in individuals who can take an unconventional approach to problem-solving, like:

1.   *Sensitivity* - the powers of perception are stretched; to see, hear, taste, touch and smell more fully or in different ways. Observations are more detailed and vivid.

2.   *Acceptance of Challenge* - problems are not seen as threats but rather challenges, an opportunity to explore the unknown.

3.   *Adaptability* - thinking is not made to conform to patterns, and patterns can be left behind. Adjustments to new developments and changes are made, where new aspects of a problem can be discovered. A problem is seen as being unique. Tried and true solutions are avoided.

4.   *Independence* - remaining true to one's beliefs to such an extent that the possible consequence of failure is accepted when the risks seem worthwhile.

5. *Abstract Thinking* - the ability to look at an object (or idea) in terms of its components; i.e., to mentally take it apart to understand the relationship between the components.

6. *Synthesizing* - to pull from the resources of various abilities, skills and knowledge and to utilize these resources to take components and recombine them in creative ways.

Barriers to Creativity

In addition to the behaviors that enable a person to think creatively, the ability to abandon mental and emotional blocks also must be present. These are barriers that prevent us from correctly or fully perceiving problems and that prevent us from arriving at the best solution. There are four major sets of blocks that hinder creativity: habitual, perceptual, cultural and emotional:

1. *Habitual Blocks*: As in "habit," these are blocks caused by resisting change and feeling comfortable with the "tried and true." We conform to the standard or norm, to what is expected of us, and we reject possible alternative solutions. We fear the exploration and manipulation of ideas.

2. *Perceptual Blocks*: These are blocks caused by the way we perceive something. We may fail to use all sensory inputs, or look from various points of view, and tend to stereotype the object or idea. We may have difficulty in isolating the problem or distinguishing between cause and effect symptoms.

3. *Cultural Blocks*: These blocks stem from our social and physical environment. We have a tendency to conform to the accepted cultural pattern. We are strongly influenced in our views by group affiliation or by someone in authority. Lack of trust among co-workers or distractions can block a group effort. We lean toward logic and pragmatism without using feelings and sensitivity as a resource.

4. *Emotional Blocks*: These blocks impose limits on our thinking. They include the fear of making a mistake, lack of accepting challenge, avoiding disorder, prejudice, anxiety and inability to relax and "sleep on it."

You should be alert to identify these barriers to creativity, especially when involved in team activities. Then you can take action to minimize them. The key is to maintain a positive outlook no matter what the problem may be. Be confident about yourself.

Creative Techniques

We have discussed the common blocks to creativity and how they can prevent full recognition of objects or ideas, and how they can also hinder the expression of ideas. Now we will examine several techniques that provide useful, creative ways to approach and solve problems. These techniques can help us increase flexibility of thinking and reduce preconceived notions.

Brainstorming

This is an excellent, practical tool for generating creative ideas. It was developed by advertising executive, Dr. Alex Osborn, in the 1930s. It is a particularly useful technique to use with groups. When using brainstorming, groups of people can achieve greater benefit than individuals because of *synergism*. This means that the product of the group is a multiple, not a sum, of the product of the individuals within the group.

Brainstorming can be used to identify both problems and solutions in a department or work group. Topics might include:

- Actual or potential problems.

- Materials, equipment, or procedures that affect production costs, quality or schedules.

- Possible causes of problems.

- Possible solutions.

The technique centers on the free flow of ideas. Members of brainstorming groups generate ideas as fast as possible ("rapid fire") and at least one member of the group makes a list of the ideas that are described in as few words as possible, usually in one to three words. Evaluation of the ideas takes place later. There are four tested rules for conducting brainstorming sessions:

✓ Criticism and evaluation are "out."

✓ Freewheeling is welcomed.

✓ Quantity is desired.

✓ Combination and improvement are sought.

Criticism & Evaluation

The major purpose of brainstorming is to generate a large number of ideas. Creativity and spontaneity will come to a halt if group members start criticizing the ideas as they are generated. Defensiveness or asking for explanations also will hinder the creative flow. When the group stops its idea generation to talk about the ideas, they leave the brainstorming phase and jump into evaluation. Criticism, evaluation and explanations are deferred until a later time.

Free Wheeling

The more impractical and wild the ideas, the better! Farfetched ideas can "trigger" ideas in others that might be more practical in thought or application.

Quantity

The odds are that the greater the number of ideas, the greater the number of useful ideas. This facilitates exploring all possibilities and deferring the evaluation of ideas until later. You can avoid explanations by keeping the ideas limited to a one or two-word description. Duplication by other team members doesn't matter. They can be sorted out later.

Combination & Improvement

Build on the ideas of other team members. Ideas can be combined to form a better or different idea. This keeps creativity flowing. A team member can periodically read back the list of ideas already generated in order to stimulate thinking about combinations, expansion or improvement.

Keeping those four rules in mind, you can follow these steps to use the brainstorming process:

1. Appoint a recorder to list all of the ideas that are generated. Better yet, appoint two recorders because ideas are generated "rapid fire" and this will ensure that all ideas are recorded.

2. Either state a specific topic to brainstorm or select several ideas and have the team rank the topics by voting as to which are most important to discuss. This can be done by the team leader who is responsible for initiating the task function of the group.

3. Team members can begin to verbalize ideas as rapidly as they can think of them. If a lull occurs after a period of time, don't evaluate the ideas. Have the recorder(s) read the list. Or, you may wish to list the ideas on a flip chart

for easy viewing. This will help to invigorate thinking.

4.   As an aid, you also can write on the flip chart the six basic questions: Who? What? Where? When? Why? How? Other idea-spurring words to help members see new connections or relationships to the topic are "manipulative verbs." Examples are: rearrange, combine, reverse, substitute, separate, add, etc. There are many more you can probably think of as well.

Attribute Listing

Another valuable creative technique is attribute listening. It is useful in generating ideas principally for products (objects), services or concepts. It works by listing all the attributes or characteristics of a product, service or concept. Once this is done, each characteristic is studied from every possible angle for ways by which it can be improved. After all the ideas are listed, no matter how fantastic or impractical, they are evaluated.

For example, if we take a simple screwdriver and list its major features: (1) to turn screws (function); (2) round steel shank, flattened wedge-shaped end, riveted wooden handle (components); (3) gray (color); (4) cylindrical (shape); (5) smooth (texture); (6) powered manually (operation); (7) torque is developed by twisting actions (force or power). We could vary each of these categories and get different types of screwdrivers.

Value Analysis

Value analysis is a creative technique used for solving cost-related problems. It is discussed in detail in a separate unit, so we will review it only briefly here. The technique is designed to identify and remove cost from a product or service, or to lower the cost (usually the cost of the function more than the cost of the part), and still provide equivalent performance and quality levels.

The basic steps are:

1.   The function or service is described in very precise terms. Each component of the product or service must have a precise description of its function.

2.   Each function is studied to determine the cost of the function. Then, each function is broken down into components, or into all the activities involved in one whole function. Costs are assigned to each component of the function and to the function as a whole.

3.   Once total costs are calculated, questions are raised regarding whether changes or substitutions can be made. If the function of the product or service is to remain the same, are there other materials or components which

can be used that are less expensive? Can weight be reduced?
Can some components be combined? Is cost proportionate to value?
Taking a detailed look at all of the functions of an operation or product,
breaking down all costs and relating all the components and major functions
to cost and value provides a means of evaluating and improving cost
effectiveness in any type of organization.

Morphological Analysis

Morphological analysis is a creative technique used primarily to generate ideas. This
is done by first defining the independent elements that may affect a problem. Once
this is done all possible combinations of these elements are listed and evaluated to
identify creative solutions. There are four steps in this process:

1. Define the problem as broadly and generally as possible.

2. Define the elements that are present in the problem.

3. Establish a matrix and enter the elements.

4. Select a combination of elements, trying to find all possible combinations.
    Then evaluate, test, modify, and develop the most practicable combinations.

For example, consider the nature of a problem or issue, and determine the common
general approaches to it. In the case of lost-time accidents, several major approaches
or elements are involved: engineering, communication, education, and motivation.
Break down each element into as many sub-elements as you can (See Figure 9-1).

In order to generate creative ideas about ways to reduce lost-time accidents, select one
item at random from each column. For example, suppose you selected "mechanical
hazards" from Column 1; "recognition awards" from Column 2; "accident statistics"
from Column 3; and "house organs" from Column 4. Then, put these four items
together to form an idea. For example, "Develop a program in which recognition
awards, such as plaques, pins, etc., are given to employees who identify and report
mechanical safety hazards to their supervisor. Publish (in the monthly house organ)
the names of these employees, together with the hazard they identified, the action
taken to correct it, and the award given."

Concentrate on generating ideas and don't worry about how practical they might be.
Evaluate how practical each might be after you have generated a number of ideas by
combining elements from each column at random.

Morphological Analysis for Safety Program

Element 1 Engineering	Element 2 Motivation	Element 3 Education	Element 4 Communication
Safety Engineers	Safety Contest	Safety Videos	Employee Meetings
Accident Investigations	Employee Participation	Safety Posters	House Organs
Safety Equipment	Discipline	On-line Safety Training	Loudspeakers
Protective Clothing	Recognition Awards	OJT	Email to Homes
Policies & Procedures	Wise Owl Club	Peer Discussions	Personal Counseling
PM Program	Saf-T-Plan	Safety Consultants	Pay Envelope Stuffers
Equipment & Design	Safety Specialists	Accident Statistics	Intra-Company Web Site
Mechanical Hazards			

Figure 9-1

SUMMARY

Everyone has creative abilities that are "underdeveloped" because of rigid thinking patterns and barriers. The most common barriers are habitual, perceptual, cultural, and emotional blocks. Creative characteristics include sensitivity, challenge acceptance, adaptability, independence, ability to abstract, and to the ability to synthesize. The removal of blocks and the utilization of these characteristics enables a more complete recognition and diagnosis of ideas and freedom and variety of idea expression.

Creativity is affected by our interaction with others. It cannot be "turned on" and made to flow from a tap, but it is possible to create an atmosphere whereby people can feel comfortable in presenting and evaluating ideas. Ideas can be encouraged both by management and by team members. When people are engaged in problem solving, an added benefit is that all receive a better understanding of the team's objectives. Enthusiasm is fostered for problem solving by the openness and acceptability of ideas generated by the various creative techniques.

The creative techniques presented in this book have valuable practical application and have been used successfully by many organizations. They lend a methodical approach to creative problem solving. This is important because the creative process is not really disorderly and chaotic. Creativity can be channeled constructively, simply by being aware that one of the human needs is self expression.

TEST & DISCUSSION QUESTIONS

1. Which sentence best describes creativity?

    ☐ a.   "Sticking with the tried and true."

    ☐ b.   "Looking at one thing and seeing another."

    ☐ c.   "Staying within the lines."

    ☐ d.   "Finding just one good solution."

2. _____ involve failure to use all sensory inputs.

    ☐ a.   Cultural blocks.

    ☐ b.   Emotional blocks.

    ☐ c.   Habitual blocks.

    ☐ d.   Perceptual blocks.

3. The rules for brainstorming include:

    ☐ a.   Criticism and evaluation are ruled out.

    ☐ b.   Freewheeling is welcome.

    ☐ c.   Quantity is desired.

    ☐ d.   All of the above.

4. _____ rapidly generates ideas and requires deferred judgement.

    ☐ a.   Morphological Analysis.

    ☐ b.   Value Analysis.

    ☐ c.   Attribute Listing.

    ☐ d.   Brainstorming.

NOTES

UNIT 9   VALUE ANALYSIS

This unit has three learning objectives. After you have completed this unit, you will have learned:

1.   What Value Analysis (VA) is.

2.   How to conduct a function analysis of a component, product or service.

3.   How to use VA to improve (lower) the cost of a component, product or service without adversely affecting quality.

CONCEPT

Value Analysis (VA), also known as Value Engineering, is a problem-solving method in which the function, or purpose, of an object, component, product or service is determined and then other ways are found by which the function (if it's really needed) can be performed at lower costs. At the same time, however, the original quality level is maintained.

VA was first developed in World War II when there was a scarcity of war-related material like metal and rubber. During that period the government rewarded people with extra ration coupons for turning in scarce war commodities like tin (from cans) and grease (from animal fat). In England, the scarcity of metal prompted the British to manufacture the Mosquito bomber out of plywood. The same function that was performed by other warplanes was duplicated but with substitute material (plywood instead of metal) and at lower cost. Quality was not sacrificed. The Mosquito was a very effective warplane. Still another example of how VA was used during that period can be found in tires. When Axis submarines cut the shipping of rubber from plantations in South America to the USA, a substitute was found - nylon and rayon tires. Not only was quality not sacrificed but it was increased, instead!

In many ways VA follows the basic concept and principals of work simplification. In work simplification the objective is to conserve material, manpower, energy, space and time. VA also has much in common with other problem-solving methods. For example, VA follows a rational or scientific process much the same as is used in decision-making and problem-solving methods in general:

1.   Identify the problem.
2.   Gather facts.
3.   Analyze the facts.
4.   Develop alternatives.
5.   Evaluate alternatives.
6.   Decide and act.

In VA, these steps have slightly different names. Also, the six VA steps together are called the VA Job Plan.

VA JOB PLAN

The VA Job Plan is a systematic way for carrying out a VA study. These steps are the:

1. Selection Phase.
2. Information Phase.
3. Function Analysis Phase.
4. Creative Phase.
5. Evaluative Phase.
6. Action Phase.

1. *Selection Phase* - This is an important step in which the VA target is carefully selected and defined as precisely as possible.

2. *Information Phase* - As many facts as possible about the target (problem) are gathered, including everything that can be found about its costs.

3. *Function Analysis Phase* - The main activity here is to define both the primary and secondary functions of what is being studied.

4. *Creative Phase* - In this phase ideas are developed about alternative ways by which the essential functions of the target can be performed.

5. *Evaluative Phase* - Alternatives are critically evaluated, the best one(s) are selected and unnecessary functions are discarded.

6. *Action Phase* - In this wrap-up phase ideas are turned into reality. Action plans are developed and solutions are implemented.

Earlier, in the unit about decision making and problem solving, you learned how to do all of the above steps except one, function analysis. This unit will concentrate on function analysis because it is unique to VA and because it affects how you perform most of the other steps or phases.

FUNCTION ANALYSIS

There are four definitions that are essential to the understanding of function analysis:

1. *Function* - Function is a characteristic that a component, product or service accomplishes which is described by two words, a verb and a noun (more on this later).

2. *Basic Function* - The primary purpose of a product or service - its main reason for being - or that which directly and essentially contributes to the primary purpose.

3. *Secondary Function* - Some purposes other than the main reason why the component, product or service exists.

4. *Function Cost* - The cost of all of the elements that together accomplish a function.

Now let's simplify those definitions through some easy-to-understand examples. First, the reason why VA users describe a function in only two words, a verb and a noun, is to keep it simple and to stimulate creativity! The more words you use to describe a function the harder it will be to determine what the main purpose of it is and the more difficult it is to be creative. Let's think of some common objects to illustrate what we mean by the word *function*. What is the main purpose, or basic function, of a chair? You might say "to sit on." But is that really the most basic function? Does that enhance our chances to be creative?

If we say that the function of a chair is "to sit on" and then look for other ways to perform the function, we will probably look for other conventional things "to sit on." But, if we recognize that the basic function of a chair is to "support weight" (a verb and a noun) then the sky is the limit as we seek other ways to perform that function. What else supports weight? Concrete blocks, rocks, tree stumps, bean bags, the floor, pilings and a lot more. Remember in brainstorming it is a lot easier to pare down a long list than it is to puff up a short one.

Try one more example. Is the basic function of a glass, or cup "To drink from?" Again that is too narrow. How about "contain matter?" Once again, we open up our scope of alternatives. A tremendous number of other objects can contain matter. In fact, you probably will think of so many that the next problem will be to cut the list down to a practical few that could perform that same function at lower cost without adversely affecting quality.

It is fairly easy to distinguish between a basic function and a secondary function. Consider paint on a wooden house. The primary or basic function is to *protect wood*. But, few people would paint their house an ugly color. Appearance is an important secondary function. Similarly, a dining room table might have as its basic function: *support weight*. But most people would be very particular about the specific style of table that they selected. "*Enhance appearance*" can, in certain cases, even be the primary function.

FUNCTION COST

In most cases, it is also fairly easy to determine function cost. In order to do so you must add up the costs of all of the elements that together make up a function. To illustrate this, let us consider a common lead pencil.

The breakdown of components of a lead pencil, together with the appropriate function analysis, is as follows:

Component	Verb	Noun
Graphite	Make	Mark
Wood	Support	Graphite
Glue	Bond	Wood
Rubber	Erase	Mark
Metal	Hold	Rubber
Paint	Enhance	Appearance
Ink	Provide	Advertising
Ink	Provide	Identification

Each of the above functions can be costed. Manufacturers of pencils know how much graphite (and thus the "make mark" function) costs. Each of the other functions can be similarly costed.

However, note that when you really think about it the very basic function of the pencil itself is to make a mark. Not all of the components of the pencil either make a mark or directly contribute toward it. In fact, only three of the seven components do, graphite, wood and glue; the latter two because, although they do not make a mark, are essential in order for that to occur. The thin, brittle graphite would break without the support of the glued pieces of wood. Thus, the make mark cost would be the sum of the cost of graphite, wood and glue for each pencil.

APPLYING VA

Here is an easy-to-use checklist that will help you to apply the principals of function analysis that you just learned. After you have function analyzed a component, product or service, ask:

1. What are the functions?

2. Which of the functions is basic?

3. Are all of the basic functions necessary?

4. What functions are so essential that they must be performed?

5. Which are the secondary functions? Eliminate as many as possible.

6. How much do these functions cost?

7. What else will perform these essential functions at less cost without adversely affecting quality?

The same principals also can apply to services that are provided and to administrative matters. Administrative Value Analysis (AVA), for example, follows the same process as it applies to things like paperwork systems, forms redundancies, and services that are provided. When using AVA make a VA Job Plan exactly as described earlier. The only difference is that you will now function analyze the administrative system or service. For forms you would determine what the basic purpose (function) is and whether there are any essential secondary functions. Two word descriptions like "record sales" or "resolve complaints" are commonly used to describe AVA functions.

Once AVA functions are identified they can be costed in the same way that it is possible to cost the function of a product or service. After this is done you simply proceed with the other phases of the VA Job Plan as above.

SUMMARY

VA is a problem-solving method in which you identify the function(s) of a component, product, or service and then determine how the essential function(s) can be performed at lower cost without adversely affecting quality.

There are six phases or steps in the VA method:

- Selection Phase.
- Information Phase.
- Function Analysis Phase.
- Creative Phase.
- Evaluative Phase.
- Action Phase.

In many ways, these phases are similar to other problem-solving systems. What distinguishes VA from other methods is *function analysis*. In VA you determine both the main (basic) purpose (function) of a component, product or service and any other secondary functions. Function costs are then determined by adding the costs of all of the elements which together compromise the function. VA functions are described in only two words, a verb and a noun.

When applying VA, you should eliminate all nonessential functions and then try to find alternative ways by which the remaining functions can be performed at lower cost but without sacrificing quality.

The term Administrative Value Analysis (AVA) is used when the VA target is a service or is part of an administrative system, like paperwork. AVA follows exactly the same basic process as is described in the VA Job Plan discussed in this unit.

TEST AND DISCUSSION QUESTIONS

1. Value Analysis (VA) is a problem solving method in which the _____ of a component, product or service is performed differently at lower cost.

    ☐ a.   Quality.

    ☐ b.   Object.

    ☐ c.   Design.

    ☐ d.   Function.

2. The six phases of VA together are called the _____.

    ☐ a.   VA Cycle.

    ☐ b.   VA Job Plan.

    ☐ c.   VA Problem-Solving System.

    ☐ d.   None of the above.

3. Following are four objects. Describe the most basic function for each, using a verb and a noun.

Object	Verb	Noun
a. Match	___	___
b. Table	___	___
c. Knife	___	___
d. Lamp	___	___

4. The cost of a function is the cost of all of the elements of the product or service.

    ☐ a.   True.

    ☐ b.   False.

NOTES

UNIT 10   CREATIVE PROBLEM SOLVING

This unit has two learning objectives. After completing this unit you will have learned:

1. What the Creative Problem-Solving (CPS) method is and how you can use it to solve cost, quality and productivity problems.

2. How CPS combines convergent and divergent thinking into a highly effective problem solving method.

Creative problem solving has proven very useful in a broad variety of situations, particularly in quality-related problems. It is creative in the sense that it offers the opportunity for open-ended or divergent thinking by making use of the creative techniques discussed earlier. This is combined with analysis, evaluation and structured or convergent thinking. Overall, it is a flexible method that can be applied to many forms of problem resolution.

CPS follows this basic 8-step model:

1. Select the problem.
2. Describe the problem.
3. Gather additional facts.
4. Set an objective.
5. Determine problem causes.
6. Develop alternative solutions.
7. Evaluate alternatives.
8. Develop an implementation plan.

STEP 1 - SELECT THE PROBLEM.

The first step in any problem-solving process is to select and define the problem. This is a very important step since all subsequent efforts are based on an accurate definition of the problem. Accuracy is a must. Whether you will be using this process as an individual or as part of a team, time energy, people, money and other resources will be involved in your efforts. You cannot afford to waste time trying to solve the wrong problem. You must focus your resources on those problems which will give you the greatest return on the resources invested. We will approach the CPS method in regard to quality problems, although it is equally effective for solving other types of organizational problems.

You begin Step 1 in the CPS process by making a list of quality improvement problems. Brainstorming is a good technique for developing this list. Once you have listed the problems, you should rank them in terms of either the negative effect they have on quality or the positive effect they will have when solved. You can use Pareto

Analysis or a similar method to rank or prioritize the problems.

Step 1 also provides for the issue of *controllability* of a target. There is little benefit in selecting a high priority target to work on if you have little, or no control over it. Consider the factor of controllability from the viewpoint of the organizational unit within which the quality improvement activity will be effected.

The value of impact and controllability is that these criteria help you to select quality improvement problems for further analysis on a rational basis. The quality problem that you will want to tackle first should be the one that has the best combination of impact and controllability. You still want to tackle the other problems but probably in descending priority order.

An example of how one quality improvement team began the CPS process will be found on page 85.

STEP 2 - DESCRIBE THE PROBLEM

Now that you have ranked the quality improvement problems in priority order, you should select the one having the best combination of impact and controllability to work on first. This is part of the refinement process which soon will lead you to defining a specific quality improvement objective.

At this point, you should have a general quality improvement problem on which you will be working. It could be scrap, waste, direct labor, materials or any other quality problem. The target probably is still broad, general and vague. It might cover many smaller categories or sub-problems. You need to be more precise in order to develop a valid and useful quality improvement objective.

One way to begin to do this is to *describe* what actually is happening now. Write a one paragraph narrative story, a verbal picture of it. Write as if you were trying to tell someone else about the problem, such as a co-worker or boss. Don't forget the details. Include who, what, when, where, how much, how often and other descriptive questions. Give specific examples whenever possible.

Next, state exactly what should be happening. Again, be as specific as possible. Then, determine the difference (variance) between what actually *is* happening and what you believe *should be* happening.

One of the benefits of describing the quality improvement problem as fully as possible is that you are setting down all of the known facts at the same time. This is necessary for further analysis. Also, the description will help you later in separating the real problem issue from its surface symptoms.

Now, study the example on page 86 to learn how our CIT moving company task team handled Step 2.

STEP 3 - GATHER ADDITIONAL FACTS

This step is essential before you can proceed to solve the problem that you have now described. If you did a thorough job in Step 2, you should have listed most of the known facts about your quality improvement target. Chances are, however, that there is some additional information about the quality improvement problem that you should obtain.

In Step 3, list the additional *facts* you should have to help you solve the quality improvement problem together with the *sources* of information for those facts. After this is done, research the information needed. When you have *answers,* write them in the space provided. Study the example on page 87 then proceed to Step 4.

STEP 4 - SET AN OBJECTIVE

You should now write a precise, measurable and realistic problem-solving objective. To do this, first review the "variance" that you described in Step 2 (refer to the example). Then write this or any major component of it as a quality improvement *objective*. In some cases, your team may find it worthwhile to combine two or more quality problems into a single objective. It is important to remember the characteristics of a valid objective. To be valid, an objective must be:

1. Precise - A broadly-worded objective will not do. It must be clear and well defined.

2. Measurable - Valid objectives must be measurable. This can be done by writing units of quantity and/or time into the objective. The best objectives specify both *quantity* (dollars, number of units, percentages, etc.) and *time* (usually beginning and ending dates).

3. Realistic - Objectives must be attainable. No one benefits if they are too tough - or too easy. Be as realistic as possible.

Lastly, you might think of two or more objectives at this point. If this does happen, determine which objective:

1. Has the greatest priority; i.e., potential for quality improvement and that,

2. Seems to be the most practical for further study.

Use this objective in the next several steps and then go back to the others and solve them using the same process. Study the example on page 88.

STEP 5 - DETERMINE PROBLEM CAUSES

You are now ready to begin to analyze the problem. In order to solve the problem, you must first determine its cause(s); i.e., *why* it exists. By determining why it exists, solutions become more visible.

You should be very careful to distinguish between symptoms of a problem and its true cause(s). For example, perhaps excessive rework can be traced to worker error. Why do they repeatedly make errors? Poor attitude? Lack of proper training? If so, why? Which is a symptom and which is a true problem root cause?

One way to determine a problem root cause is to construct a cause-effect (C-E) diagram. This provides a rational means by which you can break down a problem into components and trace its causes until you identify the real reason it exists.

Study the example on page 89 which breaks down the causes of the customer inquiry problem.

STEP 6 - DEVELOP ALTERNATIVE SOLUTIONS

Before you begin searching for alternative solutions, restudy your total fact base, review your problem finding analysis and be sure you clearly understand your objective. All of the previous steps must be fully understood by all of your CIT members; if not, now is the time for group discussion and clarification. Once this is done, you can begin to generate ideas leading to possible solutions. In our example, the CIT used the brainstorming technique.

Remember, in the brainstorming process the objective is to generate as many ideas as possible. This can be done by rapid fire idea giving. No judgements or evaluations are allowed. After your team has exhausted the list of alternative ideas, you will have sufficient time to go back, evaluate the ideas, separate the "wheat from the chaff," categorize, eliminate duplication of ideas, etc.

Also, although we are suggesting the brainstorming technique, do not forget that there are several other very useful creative techniques, such as attribute listing, morphological analysis, and value analysis for more technical problem-solving. Do not hesitate, when appropriate, to request staff specialists to provide your team with additional input or guidance.

Now, develop alternative solutions to your problem. Consider the root causes of the problem. These causes can be viewed as negative forces affecting the situation and which contribute to or fully produce the problem. Your solutions(s) should remove or lesson the problem root causes and, if possible, add new positive forces as well. Study the example on page 90. Notice that the solutions are in a simple checklist form.

STEP 7 - EVALUATE ALTERNATIVES

Whichever solution-finding technique was used you will now have several alternative solutions to consider. How can you be sure which of these is the best solution?

One way is to determine the standards or criteria for evaluation against which the alternative can be judged. There is no fixed rule for selecting evaluation criteria. The criteria may include:

- Quality of the idea.

- Returns on investment.

- Impact on employee relations.

- Acceptance probability by higher management.

- Availability of tools, equipment, skills, etc.

- Impact on the environment.

    And others.

In this step you should judge each idea, alternative possible solution, against all of the applicable evaluation criteria. Then, decide whether you want to implement the idea, modify it (if so, how?), or abandon it. After you evaluate all of the possible solutions, it will become apparent which one, or ones, should be selected. When evaluating each solution, you can use a code like the one given in the example to follow. They are rated against the criteria, ranging from "very good" to "not applicable." After they are rated against each criterion, then you can decide whether they can be fully adopted, modified, or abandoned. The comment section allows you to indicate the modifications.

The example on page 91 shows you how the model CIT evaluated their quality improvement ideas.

STEP 8 - IMPLEMENT BEST SOLUTION

Some quality improvement programs stop at the idea generation stage. In these programs, once you develop a quality improvement idea and submit it to a suggestion review committee your job is done. In our opinion, your job is not done until you have developed a plan by which the best solution to your quality problem can be implemented. We call this an Action Plan.

The Action Plan is a very useful and necessary part of the quality improvement process. It is your blueprint for action - solution implementation. The Action Plan restates the original quality improvement objective which you wrote in STEP 4 and specifically focuses on one of the solutions which you have selected to accomplish that objective (solve the problem).

In this step, solutions are transformed into reality. Responsibilities are delegated to accomplish the objective. As in the previous stages of the creative problem-solving process, each member of the team must stick by the commitment to correct the problem.

The Action Plan provides the following details which you must have for solution implementation:

1. Strategies: specific action steps which you will take to solve the problem.

2. Substrategies: detailed components of each strategy.

3. Responsibilities (RESP): the person or people who are responsible for carrying out each Strategy or Substrategy.

4. Resources: help needed from other people or departments or financial and material resources needed to put the Strategy or Substrategy into action.

5. Time: due dates for each Strategy and Substrategy.

As you prepare your Action Plan, you should be sure to coordinate the various components of it with others who will be involved. A solution is only a good intention until it is carried out in a specific manner. This is important in order to obtain commitment to the plan and ensure that all steps can be performed, when needed, by the right person with the necessary resources. After completing your plan, you should distribute a copy of it to all who are involved in putting the plan into effect or providing resource assistance for it. Then, use it as an action guide and for coordination and control purposes. Now study the example of an Action Plan that will be found on page 92.

Converting the solution (decision) into action is an important step, and requires answers to various questions. Typically, one must know who is best suited to carry out a specific task (strategies and sub-strategies). Two important and commonly overlooked questions are:

1. *Who* must know about the decision(s)?

2. Is the action to be taken within the capacity of those who must carry it out?

In other words, the CIT must anticipate how widely the solution will affect other areas of the organization. The team must investigate the adequacy of the resources of their organization and assess how their particular recommendations can be integrated with the overall continuous improvement efforts of the organization. Only then will the chances be favorable for final approval of their plan.

FORCE FIELD ANALYSIS

Once the Action Plan is complete, it should be submitted for approval. Let's suppose the plan was given to a committee, who read it over and responded:

- "It just won't work."
- "It costs too much."
- "We tried that six years ago."
- "We don't have the people."

Responses similar to these are very possible when presenting an Action Plan. The CIT must anticipate negative reactions and should be armed to handle them. One technique used to help reduce difficulties in Action Plan presentations is called Force Field Analysis. When selling an idea, precautionary measures can be taken to handle any objections that might come your way. This technique was developed to analyze goal-seeking situations. In our case, the goal is to get the Action Plan accepted. Any situation involves *driving* (positive) forces that push a situation toward acceptance. It also involves *restraining* (negative) forces that restrain the driving forces. Simply stated, there are pros and cons to any situation. Some members of a suggestion review committee may pose opposition to all or parts of the Action Plan and they may have justification for their disagreement or questions.

What can the CIT do to reduce opposition and successfully sell their Action Plan to other members of the organization? By using Force Field Analysis the team can assess the probable consequences, compare and analyze the side effects, risks and probabilities of each alternative. The team should analyze the strategies in terms of the pros and cons of each and in relation to how others within the organization may react to them. This can be done by a three-step process:

1. Examine each strategy and list all the possible areas of resistance or cons. Use a scale of 1 to 5 to indicate its relative strength.

2. Next, look at all the favorable areas of acceptance or the pros of each strategy. List them and rate them according to relative strength using a scale of 1 to 5.

3. Now the team can objectively evaluate how favorable the Action Plan is in terms of its restraining and driving forces. The final step is to shorten or eliminate the cons and lengthen or strengthen the pros.

If modification is needed, now is the time to do so before your plan is presented. The team is now armed to handle objections and accomplish the goal of acceptance.

FEEDBACK, CONTROL & FOLLOW UP

Another element of successful Action Planning is feedback. Feedback is necessary for control; to ensure that the plan is proceeding as envisioned and that it is accomplishing its objectives. This must be built into the Action Plan itself, as seen in our example of Step 8. Just as two-way communication is necessary for successful solution implementation, continuous improvement efforts require effective communication among all areas of the organization and active participation in the activities of the continuous improvement plan. Team members must go out "into the field" and be exposed to the reality of the Action Plan in progress. Only then can plan results are accurately measured and adjustments are made when the organization undergoes changes, allowing benefits to continue long after implementation.

SUMMARY

There are many methods to improve costs, quality and productivity in any type of organization. An excellent method, and one which is ideal for use by CITs, is Creative Problem Solving (CPS). This method combines highly creative techniques with the most practical features of the scientific method. CPS can easily be used by individuals or by members of a CIT to solve many different types of problems. The CPS method, as it applies to solving quality improvement problems, involves these eight steps:

1   *Identify Continuous Improvement Targets*

List continuous improvement opportunities together with the impact they have on costs and profits and their degree of controllability.

2 *Describe the Quality Improvement Target*

Write a general description of the situation or circumstances surrounding the continuous improvement target that you have decided to solve.

3 *Gather Additional Facts*

List all additional facts needed about the problem, the sources of these facts, and then research the information needed.

4 *Set an Objective*

Write a precise, measurable and realistic problem solving objective.

5 *Determine Problem Causes*

Break the problem into its various components and list probable causes.

6 *Find Solutions*

Use various creative and rational methods to develop alternative solutions.

7 *Evaluate Solutions*

Develop criteria or standards against which the alternatives can be evaluated. Evaluate them and select the best solutions for implementation.

8 *Develop an Action Plan*

Develop a detailed plan by which the best solution to the quality problem can be implemented.

The Action Plan is the actual blueprint for putting a solution into effect. It restates the original problem solving objective of STEP 4 and one of the solutions selected to solve the problem. It contains five basic parts:

1. Strategies.
2. Substrategies.
3. Responsibilities.
4. Resources.
5. Time.

The activities related to these parts must be coordinated with others who will be involved in solution implementation.

The presentation of the plan is likely to be more effective if anticipated problems are analyzed and remedied by using Force Field Analysis. By examining pros and cons of each strategy, the team can strengthen the driving forces and reduce the restraining forces for successful acceptance. Two-way communication is vital to all aspects of this process so that ideas and responsibilities are fully understood.

The CPS method can be applied to any activity of any organization. Size, financial resources and elaborate systems and procedures are not prerequisites for effective continuous improvement. By using this eight-step method even organizations with limited resources and personnel can reap rewards which will benefit both the organization and its employees, alike.

Step 1   **Identify the Problems**

The first cost, quality or productivity improvement target that you select for further analysis should be the one that has the combination of high impact and high controllability. In this case the CIT selected *Delays to Customer Inquiries*.

Improvement Target or Problem	Impact	Control
Excessive photocopier usage	2	H
Excessive and unauthorized telephone usage	2	S
Waste office supplies	3	S
Coffee break abuses	3	S
Poor facility maintenance/cleaning service	3	N
Delays to customer inquiries	**1**	**H**
Cluttered office decor	3	H
Incorrectly archived material	1	S
Forms inventory storage errors	2	S
Redundant forms distribution	2	H
Operating manual errors	3	H
Excessive shipping charges	2	S
Postage meter abuse	2	H
Unproductive meetings	1	S
Network crashes	2	H

Figure 10-1

Step 2   **Describe the Problem**

After selecting the problem issue that has the combination of high impact and also high controllability you should clearly describe what is happening, what should be happening and what the variance or gap between the two is.

Diagnostic Questions	Description
A. What is happening now? Who is involved? When or how often does it happen? How much does it cost? How long does it take? Where does it happen?	Customers frequently call the Customer Care Department to learn the exact time of delivery at their new location. It now takes as long as 2 days for a response to their inquiries. Average response time is 24 hours. As a result of this problem estimated lost business is approximately $425,000 annually.
B. What should be happening?	We should be able to respond to customers in no more than 2-3 hours.
C. What is the variance or "gap?"	The variance or gap averages 21-22 hours.

Figure 10-2

Step 3   **Gather the Facts**

In column A list all of the additional facts that you must have in order to solve the cost improvement problem that you selected for further study. List the likely sources for these facts in Column B. When you have researched the facts write the answers in Column C.

A. Additional Facts	B. Source	C. Answers
1. Number of customer inquiries per day or week.	Customer care supervisor.	Averages 9 per day.
2. Why dispatchers do not respond to customer inquiries more promptly?	Dispatcher supervisor and dispatchers; possibly traffic department manager, also.	Heavy work load to some extent but mostly because of low priority compared with other tasks. Also, dispatchers think that their response time is good.
3. The work load and priority of customer care responses to inquiries.	Customer care supervisor; possibly sales manager and customer care employees.	High priority work load is moderate to heavy but should not interfere with response time.
4. Method used to convey information between dispatchers and customer care staff.	Customer care and dispatcher supervisors.	Interoffice email, telephone, some personal contact.
5. Method used by dispatchers to obtain status data.	Observation.	Computer terminals.
6. How long the "best" customer care employees take to respond to inquiries.	Customer care supervisor and observation.	Less than 2 hours (2 employees out of 12).

Figure 10-3

87

Step 4   **Set an Objective**

Write a precise, measurable and realistic cost improvement objective for the most promising target that you selected in Step 2.

Cost Improvement Objective	
Precise, measurable and realistic cost improvement objective.	To improve response time to customer inquiries about the exact date of delivery of household goods to their new location from an average of 24 hours to not more than 3 hours within the next 60 days.

Figure 10-4

Step 5   Determine Problem Causes

In this step you can use cause-effect analysis to help you determine the problem root causes.

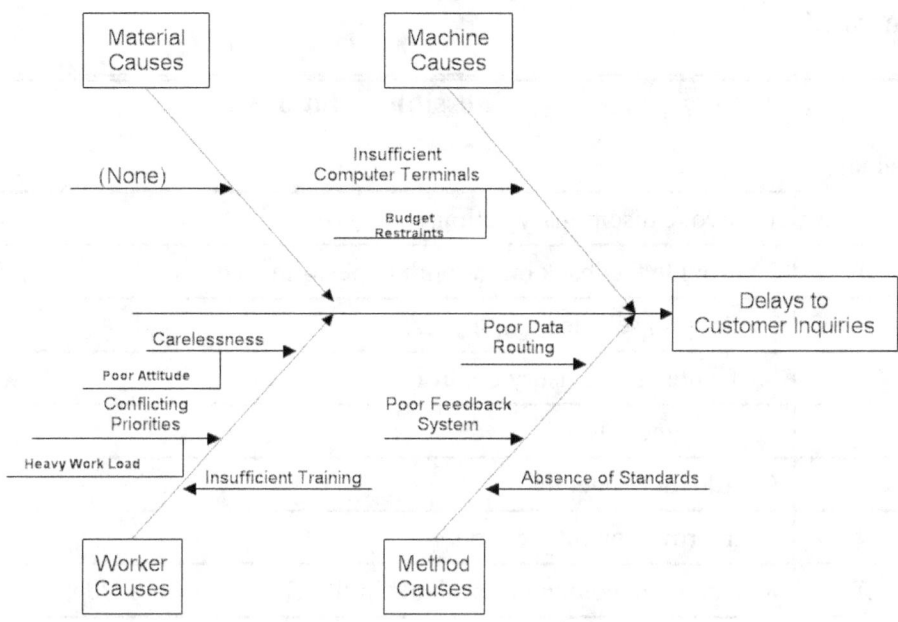

Figure 10-5

Step 6   **Find Solutions**

Use both creative and traditional methods to generate possible solutions to the problem. Brain storming, morphological analysis and value analysis are among the ways that will help you to develop alternative solutions. Then select the best for further evaluation. Below is an example of the alternative solutions that the CIT generated.

Possible Solutions	
Select	
	1. Invoke disciplinary action.
X	2. Provide feedback on individual performance.
	3. Counsel selected employees.
	4. Tighten supervisory control
X	5. Set standards.
	6. Add more people.
	7. Improve communication.
X	8. Add more computer terminals in the Customer Care Dept.
X	9. Communicate problem more clearly to all employees.
X	10. Develop rewards program for speedy response times.
X	11. Improve dispatcher and Customer Care employees training.
	12. Revise operating procedures.
	13. Revise routing forms for inquiries.
	14. Refer customer inquiries directly to dispatchers.

Figure 10-6

Step 7   **Evaluate Solutions**

Use an evaluation matrix similar to the one in Figure 10-7 below to help you select the best solution(s). In Column A list the possible solutions that you circled for further consideration in Step 6. Determine the criteria (standards) by which you can evaluate the true value of each alternative solution and list them in Column B. In Column C indicate your decision for each alternative solution. Then, in Column D, note any ways in which the possible solution might have to be modified.

Evaluate each possible solution by using the following rating code: VG=Very Good, G=Good, F=Fair and N/A=Not applicable. Select the best solution(s) for implementation.

A. Possible solutions		Cost of idea	Impact on morale	Time to implement	Management acceptance	Effect on objective		Adopt	Modify	Abandon	D. Comments
		B. Criteria						C. Check decisions			D. Comments
Set standards	1.	VG	F	G	VG	VG		x			Already done via objective.
Add terminals in customer service.	2.	F	G	G	G	G			x		Study to see how many are needed.
Communicate problem better.	3.	VG	G	VG	VG	F			x		Incorporate with 1, 2, and 5.
Develop motivation plan.	4.	G	G	F	G	G		x			
Improve training.	5.	G	F	F	F	F			x		
Provide feedback.	6.	VG	G	G	VG	VG		x			Combine with 2.

Figure 10-7

91

         # Develop An Action Plan

Prepare a detailed action plan by which you can implement the best alternative solution(s) that you selected in Step 7. Write a separate action plan if there is more than one solution that you have selected to remedy the problem.

To improve response time to customer inquiries from an average of 24 hours to not more than 3 hours within the next 60 days.

- Communicate problem and standard.
- Develop feedback and motivation plan.

Strategies	Responsible Individual	Substrategies	Responsible Individual	Resources	Time
1. Design feedback checklist for customer service and dispatching personnel.	T.P.	1. Meet with customer service and dispatching supervisors.	T.P.	Forms control systems department	9/15
		2. Draft form.	L.R.	Reproduction department	
		3. Send out for review and approval.	L.R.		
		4. Print supply.			
2. Design nonfinancial recognition plan.	T.P.	1. Review alternate plans.	T.P.	Employee relations department	9/23
		2. Select and cost best plan.	T.P.		
		3. Prepare plan procedures.	L.R.		
		4. Obtain approvals.	T.P.		
3. Present program to managers and supervisors.	J.W.	1. Arrange for meeting room.	S.C.	Secretarial and reproduction department	9/29
		2. Schedule personnel.			
		3. Prepare AVs.			
4. Hold general meeting with dispatchers and customer service personnel to discuss problem, explain objective (standard), and discuss feedback and motivation plan.	J.W.	1. Arrange for meeting room.	S.C.	Secretarial and reproduction department	10/3
		2. Schedule personnel.			
		3. Prepare handouts.			

Figure 10-8

Because of the nature of Units 10 and 12 a test for those units has been intentionally omitted.

NOTES

Unit 11　　　　　　**REPORTS TO MANAGEMENT**

This unit has three learning objectives. After completing this unit you will have learned:

1.　How to prepare for a report of CIT activities to management.

2.　What kind of resistance to your CIT's ideas you might encounter.

3.　Key elements of the presentation process.

Continuous Improvement Team members at some point in time will be required to periodically inform management about certain aspects of their assignment. For example, if a CIT is ready to implement an action plan, a presentation may be needed to explain the team's efforts and the plan to management. Other purposes of reports and presentations may concern:

- Problem issues where a solution could not be found and alternative actions may need to be taken.

- Communication to management regarding any issue, whether it be data analysis, potential problems, grievances and complaints or ideas for improving profits.

- Status reports of ongoing projects or programs.

- Clarification of ideas or written reports to help prevent misunderstanding.

- Details of Action Plans.

There are probably many other reasons that you can think of when it is necessary for presentations to be made to management. The point is that as a member of a CIT you are likely to be involved in one or more of these presentations.

A presentation usually takes the form of a meeting.　As in any meeting, one advantage is that information can be communicated to many people at the same time. Also, meetings allow feedback and group participation which may be instrumental in achieving acceptance of recommendations.

Preparation

In an earlier unit, you learned that the success of a meeting if often determined by how well you prepare for it. Let us now briefly review some of the guidelines for successful meeting preparation.

Determine Your Objective: What is it that you specifically want to have accomplished at your meeting?

Decide Who Should Attend: Make sure you invite the right people. Who should know about your report.

Schedule the Meeting: Try to work out a schedule that is most convenient for all who will attend.

Prepare an Agenda: As mentioned before, this is a very important part of the preparation process. List exactly the order in which the subjects are to be discussed and who is to discuss them. If you are seeking approval or the support of management, how you present your information may determine its approval or rejection.

Arrange the Physical Setting: This includes comfort, accessibility, availability of equipment, seating arrangement and size of the meeting room. You may wish to make a checklist of "extras" that will give your presentation more impact, such as audio-visual equipment, flip chart, handouts, samples, etc. Also, be sure to arrange for the needs of any handicapped participants.

Two other aspects of meetings that you should be aware of during the preparation process are the content of the data and the process of how the data are to be used. The content, or what the data actually says, provides information to the group. It is vital that data be valid and verifiable therefore you should provide information about how the data was obtained. This will help your audience understand it better and will also help gain their acceptance of its validity. The nature of the presentation and the management members that attend will determine how the data are used; i.e., how the group goes about and works with what is presented to them. Certain presentations, especially those related to quality improvement, may focus on data that pertains to management policies and practices as well as operational procedures.

Management may come to the meeting with certain feelings that will affect the meeting process or outcome. It is common that resistance to a CIT's ideas might be encountered. For example, there might be resistance to a recommended improvement due to personal fears or lack of a clear understanding of the need for improvement.

Resistance may take several forms:

Fear Of Something New

Certain people may feel that a new program will "rock the boat" or threaten their positions.

Fear Of New Responsibility

Those management members who must take part in the program may not be sure that they can put the improvement into effect or that the program can produce positive, measurable results.

Misunderstanding Of Objectives

Members may feel that a continuous improvement program indicates that they have not been doing their job properly and they may take personal offense. Or, they may not feel a program is even necessary if the company is currently profitable.

If your team is aware of these types of resistance, you will be in a better position to prevent their occurrence and to handle them properly if they arise. That is not to say that your audience will be negative. Many may attend the meeting who are excited, supportive and full of positive energy. They may anticipate and desire constructive change. In total, there may be a mixture of possible reactions, which is why the process of working with the data is very important.

Presentation Process

Prior to the time of your presentation, it would be a good idea to do a "practice run" to work out any weaknesses before it is formally presented. This would also include setting up any visual aids such as charts or graphs. Your presentation should also be geared to those who are attending; in other words, use language that management can understand. Speak in terms of costs, quality, delivery time, schedules, safety, etc. Knowing what resistance certain people may have and what questions they may ask, will help you to assemble proper data and then present it when necessary at strategic points in the report.

The presentation is a team effort in both formulation, preparation and delivery. The team's attitude must be positive and must be conveyed in that manner. Realize that questions and resistance may occur, but don't let your presentation become ineffectual because of the assumption that management is not concerned. Make them concerned. Give your presentation impact by few suggested guidelines:

1. Be punctual. Start on time.

2. Introduce team members who will take part in the presentation.

3. Explain the problem or purpose of the meeting.

4.   Give a brief outline (agenda) of what is to be covered and how. Then as you follow your agenda, give specific examples and detailed data. This is especially important if the chief executive is attending.

5.   Be enthusiastic and be sensitive to the interests of those attending. Handle questions as efficiently as possible from the information you've prepared in advance. If another team member is better equipped to give an answer, then direct the question to him or her.

6.   Follow your agenda and use your visual aids to emphasize key points.

7.   If the content of this meeting is a status report, then tell your audience what changes will be made and what problems you will tackle next. Indicate when the next meeting will be.

8.   Encourage questions.

9.   Close the meeting. Thank everyone for attending.

TEST & DISCUSSION QUESTIONS

1. Which of the following is not a valid purpose of a CIT report to management?

   ☐ a. Problem issues where a solution could not be found and alternative actions may need to be taken.

   ☐ b. Communication to management regarding any issue, whether it be data analysis, potential problems, grievances and complaints or ideas for improving profits.

   ☐ c. Routine disagreements among members of the CIT.

   ☐ d. Status reports of ongoing projects or programs.

2. In preparing for a successful report to management about CIT activities the CIT should:

   ☐ a. Determine their agenda.

   ☐ b. Decide who should attend.

   ☐ c. Make appropriate physical arrangements.

   ☐ d. All of the above.

3. In most cases as long a CIT prepares properly for a meeting with management it is unlikely that they will encounter any form of resistance to their ideas.

   ☐ a. True.

   ☐ b. False.

4. When presenting a CIT's analysis and recommendations it is important that the CIT members and presentation leaders remain unemotional and project a neutral sense of interest.

   ☐ a. True

   ☐ b. False

NOTES

Unit 12   CIT PROGRAM & MODEL MASTER PLAN

PROGRAM OBJECTIVES

The following objectives are common to most Continuous Improvement Team programs. Specific objectives are established within each individual organization.

1.   To develop an attitude among all employees which makes active, continuous cost, quality and productivity improvement a regular part of planned management and work activities at all levels of the organization.

2.   To achieve increased organization effectiveness and profitability by establishing a work climate that is characterized by:

- continuous improvement,

- full attainment of customer expectations and satisfaction,

- teamwork,

- problem solving,

- measurement and analysis of work processes.

3.   To involve all employees in the creative and innovative processes that best facilitate cost, quality and productivity improvement.

4.   To establish an environment in which management and non-management employees work collaboratively toward the attainment of a common goal, ensuring the continued strength and vitality of the organization.

COMMITMENT

The first, and perhaps the most important, step in the CIT process is to ensure that top management is fully committed to the concept of continuous improvement and, in particular, to a Continuous Improvement Team program. Continuous improvement can only be achieved when the proper time, material and people resources are allocated to this effort. Further, although a CIT program is designed to produce near term as well as long range results, top management must adopt a long-term perspective. In

101

most cases problems do not arise overnight. Nor can most be solved that quickly. Serious problems may have complex causes which require a longer time to resolve (reference Deming's "common causes" versus "special causes"). In any event, top management, the policy level of the organization, most visibly and enthusiastically demonstrate their personal and collective commitment to continuous improvement in order for your CIT program to achieve optimum success.

OVERVIEW

The Continuous Improvement Team program begins with top management's determination to achieve total quality performance. Once this commitment is obtained top management appoints a CIT Policy Team that will be responsible for the implementation and ongoing maintenance of the CIT program. Following are the principal components of the CIT program.

Assessment

A preliminary analysis should be conducted within your organization to collect data about the various human, technical and administrative systems that can impact on a total quality team program. The total quality climate should be evaluated, prospective CIT targets must be identified and the leadership and team skills necessary to successfully implement a CIT program should be assessed. Data are usually collected via structured assessment instruments, personal interviews, observation and by a review of relevant performance data.

Planning

A CIT Policy Team is then appointed to establish program objectives, determine the structure and scope of the program, assign responsibilities and monitor results. This team consists of senior level managers who, for the purpose of this project, report to the senior executive of your organization. The team also modifies the model CIT Master Plan presented in this work to the specific needs and circumstances of the individual organization.

Continuous Improvement Teams

The CIT Policy team selects priority cost, quality and productivity improvement targets and appoints matrix type task teams which are assigned problem solving responsibility for these issues. Initially from 2 to 4 pilot Continuous Improvement Teams are appointed. After the pilot phase has been successfully completed the program is expanded to a level that is practicable for each individual organization. In most cases 10% to 15% of an organization's employees are actively involved on CITs at any particular time.

Training

CIT team leaders and team members are thoroughly trained in CIT methods and techniques. Emphasis is placed on team building, communication improvement and in the development of creative problem solving skills. In most cases the requisite training can be accomplished in approximately 24 class hours. The training program is highly participative in nature and focuses on learning through practical application.

Problem Solving

After the completion of training the CITs begin working on quality problems within their assigned target areas. They identify specific opportunities for continuous improvement, set realistic, measurable improvement goals and proceed to tackle priority issues using their newly developed problem solving skills. During this entire phase continuous coordination is maintained with the CIT Policy Team which monitors the progress of the CITs and reviews and approves their action recommendations.

Support Systems

The CIT program is supported by enhanced organization communication and recognition systems (the latter focusing principally on non-financial recognition) that are designed to obtain enthusiastic employee acceptance and commitment to the program. Technical support systems further ensure the collaboration and coordination that is necessary throughout the entire problem solving effort.

DETAILED OPERATION

1. **Assessment**

    A preliminary analysis is conducted to develop the data base necessary for implementation of a successful CIT program. Although there are several activities associated with the preliminary analysis, the principal focus is on data obtained through a structured assessment instrument proprietary to Talico that has been specifically designed to evaluate an organization's total quality climate.

    The assessment is based on composite criteria derived from the concepts advocated by quality experts such as Joseph M. Juran, W. Edwards Deming and Philip R. Crosby. The instrument focuses on the following eight total quality dimensions:

    - Quality Processes
    - Quality Results
    - Human Resource Utilization

- Teamwork
- Communication & Information
- Customer Focus
- Continuous Improvement
- Management & Leadership

The assessment data will help to identify organizational strengths and weaknesses with respect to a continuous improvement effort. Once these data are assessed it may be helpful to further define possible cost, quality and productivity improvement targets. In order to accomplish this you may want to collect and evaluate information concerning the following quality impact factors:

- Age and condition of facilities and equipment.
- Facilities layout and utilization.
- Quality standards and levels.
- Work force efficiency and utilization.
- Technical processes vs. state-of-the-art technology.
- Production/inventory control/material handling systems.
- Budgets and standard cost data.
- Recruitment, selection and training procedures.
- Turnover and absenteeism data.
- Safety statistics.
- Quality improvement consciousness, knowledge and skills.
- Economic awareness and cost consciousness.
- Organization goals, objectives and policies.
- Performance management systems and procedures.
- Communication systems.
- Quality of work life systems.
- Management and supervisory skill levels.

Most of the data for the above should be readily available via observation, personal interviews, the use of management and supervisory skills assessment instruments and a review of relevant statistical data. The data collected during this phase must be evaluated in the context of developing a CIT program. There are several issues that should be considered at this stage.

a. How ready is the organization for a CIT program? Is there anything that must be done before a CIT program can be implemented. For example, is top management's commitment to total quality clearly understood by all employees?

b. Are all of the resources that you will need in order to implement a CIT program available internally? If not will you need the assistance of outside resources such as consultants?

c. Based upon the data that you have collected what are the most urgent quality improvement target areas? What is their respective priority?

d. What is realistic and attainable in terms of probable results considering all of the factors associated with the preliminary analysis?

e. What type of support systems will you need to optimize the success of your CIT program? Communication? Recognition and rewards?

2. **Planning**

In large part, the success of any program depends upon how well it is planned. There is no substitute for careful and thorough planning. Planning for the CIT is the responsibility of the CIT Policy Team. A model CIT Master Plan that will give you guidelines for developing your own master plan is included later in this unit. This is a very important document because it will serve as the blueprint for your whole program. Please study the model carefully.

3. **Continuous Improvement Teams**

As provided in the CIT Master Plan, Continuous Improvement Teams are appointed by the CIT Policy Team. CITs differ very considerably from quality circles and many other types of employee involvement task teams. One major difference is that the CIT program is a management driven, management led program in which employees are encouraged to participate. However, it is management, exercising its responsibility to direct the activities of the organization, that determines such elements as the scope of the program, extent of employee involvement, quality problems to be solved, etc. Unlike quality circles and certain other similar employee involvement programs, in the CIT program the "tail" does not "wag the dog."

Another reason why the CIT program is successful is because the program focuses on bringing the most effective combination of problem solving skills to bear on each quality improvement target area; no matter what level or function of the organization may be involved. Because of this CITs are matrix structured. In contrast, quality circles are homogeneous in nature being comprised of employees from the same work unit who themselves, not management, decide what quality targets should be tackled.

Before appointing a CIT the CIT Policy Team must first determine which quality target areas have the greatest priority. Data from the Assessment phase is used as the basis for this decision. The Policy Team then selects a priority target and determines what skills within the organization are needed in order to solve that problem. For example, if a company has identified a serious

105

problem in providing on-time deliveries to customers it might appoint a CIT of the skills composition below to solve the problem:

PROBLEM: Failure to meet customers needs and expectations regarding on-time product deliveries.

CIT Team: Sales Manager
Customer Service Supervisor
Customer Service Representative (1)
Shipping Supervisor
Shipping Hourly Employee (1)
Traffic Hourly Employee (1)
Production Control Expediter (1)
Quality Assurance Group Leader (1)

As a general rule at least 30% to 40% of a CIT should be appointed from management levels.

4.   **Training**

Continuous education, training and skill development are primary criteria of continuous cost, quality and productivity improvement. In this regard it is critical that CIT members and leaders be thoroughly trained in all CIT program methods and techniques. The ten principal units of this book appropriately cover the key skills that are required for the CIT program.

5.   **Problem Solving**

Regular CIT meetings and problem solving activities commence immediately after the completion of team training. CITs set their own schedule of meetings within the time parameters that have been assigned them by the CIT Policy Team for the completion of their assignments. In most cases CITs meet once or twice a week for 1 ½ to 2 hours per session.

6.   **Support Systems**

When the CIT Policy Team determines team assignments it also makes arrangements for technical and other support advisory to be made available upon request to the various CITs. For example, during the course of problem solving it may be necessary for a CIT to obtain information or assistance from other functions of the organization that are not represented on the CIT, e.g., from finance, marketing, design engineering, human resources, etc. In most cases a designated representative from these support departments or functions is appointed and is familiarized with the CIT program. When called upon for assistance this person serves as a temporary ad hoc CIT member.

Model CIT Master Plan

A.   Background

In 2008 the ABC Division of XYZ Company was faced with the third consecutive year of declining sales and a resulting profit loss. Senior management determined that there was no single factor that was the cause of this problem. Rather, the declining state of profitability was due to several factors related to costs, quality and productivity. In January, 2009 the Company established a profit improvement objective targeted at a savings of $1,669,000 on an estimated $49,000,000 cost of sales. The program was aimed primarily at achieving savings on the cost of materials, labor, shipping and burden. By March 31, 2009 savings had already achieved 26% of the 2009 target. The momentum of the cost improvement program seemed to be accelerating and projections were optimistic. However, by June 30, 2009 although more than 50% of the cost improvement target had been achieved, it became clear that the decline in sales continued.

Further analysis by management determined that the principal reason sales were declining was because the Company's product line no longer commanded the respect among customers, and indeed within the entire industry, that they once enjoyed. Instead, customers were being increasingly attracted to foreign-made products which not only were priced lower but, more important, were of higher, more consistent quality. It was obvious, therefore, that the Company's problem was not limited to costs or productivity but rather concerned the total quality performance of the organization.

During the balance of 2009 key members of senior management, and other key managers, attended several quality workshops and seminars. As a result of the information obtained at these programs and with a firm determination to regain the Company's position as a leader in its industry, senior management made and emphatically expressed a resolve and commitment to achieve total quality improvement.

It became clear that in order to achieve total quality performance a long term collaborative effort involving all employees of the Company was necessary. Because of this management has decided to implement a Continuous Improvement Team program with the intent of obtaining the active involvement of employees in the various processes by which significant quality improvement can be achieved. The following plan establishes the basis for organizing, stimulating, evaluating, recording and recognizing the quality improvement effort of this program and sets forth the methods and procedures by which the program can be implemented.

B.   Mission Statement

It is the general purpose and intent of this program to

- develop an attitude of increased quality consciousness among all employees in order to fully meet the needs and expectations of our customers and to aid the Company in achieving its profit objectives,

- make total quality performance a regular part of planned management, supervisory and employee work activities,

- promote team building and participation by employees at all organization levels,

- establish a process by which improvement can be measured and credited.

C.   Objectives

Near-Term

1.   To meet or exceed established quality goals for FY 2010.

2.   To implement the CIT program no later than August 16, 2010 with components of that program to be implemented as scheduled below:

(a)   Administration of a Total Quality Management Climate Survey during the week of February 4, 2010.

(b)   Management review of survey data by February 28, 2010.

(C)   Assessment of additional total quality performance related data by February 28, 2010.

(D)   Selection of pilot quality improvement targets and appointment of pilot teams by March 8, 2010.

(e)   Final draft of communication and recognition plans by March 8, 2010.

(f)   Training of not less than 3 CIT pilot teams (members and leaders) by March 15, 2010.

(g)   Critique of pilot team projects by June 30, 2010.

108

(h) Full implementation of the CIT program involving 10% to 15% of the employee population actively participating on CITs by July 31, 2010.

3. To conduct a formal review and critique of program effectiveness by August 30, 2011 and annually thereafter, including the administration of annual TQM surveys.

4. To qualify for the Malcolm Baldrige National Quality Award by FY 2011.

C. Method

The general method by which these objectives can be accomplished is to establish Continuous Improvement Teams which will be trained and assigned to company-wide quality improvement problem-solving responsibilities. The teams will consist of management and non-management employees from various organization levels and functions, depending upon the general nature of the quality improvement issues which they are assigned.

D. Structure

1. CIT Policy Team

The CIT Policy Team will be appointed by the Division Manager. Initial membership of this team will consist of the following:

a. Operations Manager (Permanent Chairperson).

b. Technical Systems Manager.

c. Accounting Manager.

d. Employee Relations Manager

e. CIT Coordinator (ad hoc).

Membership of this team except for the permanent chairperson, will rotate annually.

Responsibilities of the CIT Policy Team are as follows:

a. Determine program goals and objectives.

b. Assign areas of CIT activity.

c. Assign team membership and leadership.

d. Evaluate team recommendations.

e. Recommend quality improvement action to the division Manager.

f. Determine recognition methods and credits.

g. Review and critique program progress.

Note: Implementation of quality improvements shall be the responsibility of the appropriate line manager.

2. CIT Coordinator

A CIT Coordinator will be appointed by the CIT Policy Team, subject to approval by the Division Manager. This assignment will be rotated annually and will carry the following responsibilities:

a. Serve as an internal consultant to the CITs.

b. Coordinate team training and program communication.

c. Coordinate quality improvement recommendations, approval and implementation.

d. Coordinate the activities of the various teams.

e. Coordinate the measurement of results and recognition activities.

3. Continuous Improvement Teams

CITs are appointed by the CIT Policy Team. Membership on CITs is heterogeneous in nature consisting of a cross-functional and cross-hierarchal representation of employees, depending on the nature of assigned quality improvement target areas. A management level employee is appointed as team leader for each CIT. The responsibility of the team leader is to facilitate problem solving and full participation among all team members, but not to "direct" CIT activities in the traditional manner in which line authority is exercised.

Responsibilities of the CITs are as follows:

a. Identify specific opportunities for quality improvement within assigned target areas.

b. Generate and develop quality improvement ideas, including obtaining suggestions from other employees in the members' regular work units.

c. Screen and evaluate quality improvement ideas for those which are most practicable.

d. Develop recommendations for the implementation of quality improvement ideas to the extent possible.

e. Assist in the implementation of quality improvements if requested.

E. CIT CONCEPTS

1. Definition

A "quality improvement" shall mean any improvement in technology, systems, organization or in human elements which increases the performance, reliability and consistency of a product or service. The value of any individual quality improvement is represented by the annualized value of the difference between the contribution to profitability of the improvement and the contribution to profitability that would have existed under normal circumstances if the improvement had not been made.

2. Quality Improvement Target Areas

Following are the four major areas which will be targeted for quality improvement in this program:

a. *Technology*: The technological processes of the organization, the products and services, production operations, equipment, facilities, engineering, etc.

b. *Systems*: Methods, inventory and production control, data processing, financial and other technical and administrative systems.

c. *Organization*: Structure, reporting relationships, demographic data, history of operations, functional interrelationships, etc.

d. *Human Resource Utilization*: Knowledge, skills, attitudes, beliefs, motivation, contribution and performance of employees at all organizational levels.

3. Recognition

a. Acknowledgment of quality improvement suggestions shall be made as promptly as possible. In general individual suggestions should be

111

acknowledged within one week and team recommendations within two weeks.

    b. Formal recognition of a quality improvement suggestion or recommendation shall be made when the quality improvement is put into practice.

    c. Recognition for quality improvement suggestions and recommendations shall be based on non-financial criteria; e.g., public recognition at quarterly meetings, in the house organ, recognition dinners, etc.

4. Budgets and Targets

    a. The CIT Policy Team will develop a formula for determining a return on investment rate for the annual CIT budget.

    b. The overall CIT budget will be set annually by the CIT Policy Team.

    c. The CIT Policy Team will assign general quality improvement targets to each team. Within the general target area each team will have the latitude to set priorities, objectives, etc.

5. CIT Program Administration

    a. CITs will submit recommended projects to the CIT Policy Team. A copy of these recommendations will be sent to the CIT Coordinator.

    b. CITs will submit monthly reports to the CIT Policy Team in which the following information is provided:

        (1) Dates and attendance list of team meetings.

        (2) Number and status of active projects at end of each month.

        (3) Estimated value of implemented quality improvements to date.

        (4) Other relevant information as appropriate.

    c. The CIT Policy Team will provide monthly reports to the Division Manager summarizing the various team reports.

    c. All quality improvements that require capital expenditures or variance from budget must first be approved by the Division Manager.

d. CIT program results should be communicated among the work force as broadly as possible. The actual format to be used will be determined by the CIT Policy Team.

NOTES

Bibliography

1. Brown, Mark Graham, Baldridge Award Winning Quality, How to Interpret the Malcolm Baldridge Award Criteria, White Plains, NY, Quality Resources, 1991.

2. Deming, W. Edwards, Out of the Crisis, Cambridge, MA., MIT Center for Advanced Educational Services, 1982-2000.

3. Kinlaw, Dennis C., Team Managed Facilitation, Critical Skills for Developing Self-sufficient Teams, San Diego, Pfieffer & Company, 1993.

4. Likert, Rensis and Seashore, Stanley, "Making Cost Control Work," Harvard Business Review, pp. 96-107, November-December, 1963.

5. Miles, Lawrence D., Techniques of Value Analysis and Engineering, 2d ed., New York, McGraw-Hill, 1972.

6. Osborn, Alex, Your Creative Power, New York, Dell, 1961.

7. Richardson, Wallace J., Cost Improvement, Work Simplification, and Short Interval Scheduling, Reston, VA., Reston Publishing Company, Inc., 1976.

8. Swanson, Richard A., Analysis for Improving Performance, Tools for Diagnosing Organizations and Documenting Workplace Expertise., San Francisco, Berrett-Koehler Publishing, 1994.

9. Tagliaferri, Louis E., Creative Cost Improvement for Managers, New York, John Wiley & Sons, Inc., 1981.

10. Zwichy, F., Discovery, Invention, Research Through the Morphological Approach, New York, Macmillian, 1969.

APPENDIX
TEST ANSWERS

Unit	Question	Answer	
1	1	b.	False.
	2	b.	False.
	3	d.	All of the above.
	4	d.	None of the above.
2	1	b.	False.
	2	b.	False.
	3	a.	True.
	4	a.	True.
3	1	a.	Relations between employees and management are strengthened.
	2	b.	Making decisions.
	3	c.	Identify the problem.
	4	b.	Team members are open-minded. and flexible when looking at and weighing information.
4	1	a.	Information sharing and processing.
	2	a.	Know your objective.
	3	d.	All of the above.
	4	c.	To share information.
5	1	d.	All of the above.
	2	b.	Decide what facts are needed.
	3	b.	False.
	4	a.	Pie Charts.
6	1	b.	False.
	2	c.	What data is required.
	3	d.	Periods of time.
	4	b.	False.
7	1	d.	Root cause
	2	b.	Effect
	3	b.	False
	4	c.	List the process or operation in sequence.

Unit	Question	Answer	
8	1	b.	"Looking at one thing and seeing another."
	2	d.	Perceptual blocks.
	3	d.	All of the above.
	4	d.	Brainstorming.
9	1	d.	Function.
	2	b.	VA Job Plan.
	3	a.	Produce heat.
		b.	Support weight.
		c.	Separate material.
		d.	Provide illumination.
	4	b.	False.
10	N/A	N/A	
11	1	c.	Personal disagreement is generally not an appropriate subject for a CIT report to management.
	2	d.	All of the above.
	3	b.	False. In fact, many forms of resistance might be encountered.
	4	b.	False. The team should present its findings and recommendations in an enthusiastic manner.
12	N/A	N/A	

www.ingramcontent.com/pod-product-compliance
Lightning Source LLC
Chambersburg PA
CBHW081132170526
45165CB00008B/2642